FOR GRADES 3·4

HOW TO GET BETTER TEST SCORES

on Elementary School Standardized Tests

GRADES 3-4

Editor: Jeri Hayes

Design and Production: Lynda Banks Design

Copyright © 1991 by Planned Productions Incorporated

ISBN: 0-679-82108-2

Manufactured in the United States of America

10 9 8 7 6 5 4 3 2 1

Random House New York

Table of Contents

LANGUAGE ARTS
Keeping Track

MATH

Keeping Track

Table of Contents *(continued)*

Questions and Answers About Using This Book

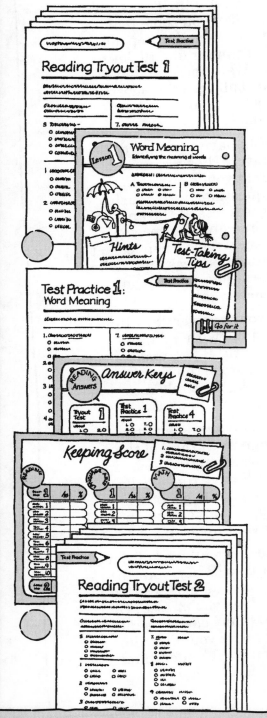

Why is this book so BIG?

Because it's three books in one! Each part gives you practice in a different subject: Reading, Language Arts, and Math.

Do I have to begin with Reading?

No. You can begin with any one of the three parts.

When I have picked a part to start on, how do I start?

Start with Tryout Test 1 for that part. The time needed for the Tryout Test is shown at the top of the first test page.

How do I check my answers?

Find the Answer Keys in the back of the book. When you have totaled the number of questions you got correct, record your score on the test page and on the Keeping Score chart in the back of the book. The page numbers are in the Table of Contents.

Must I do all the lessons in one part of the book before going on to another part?

No. Just be sure to take Tryout Test 1 in each part before you do the lessons in that part. Keep track of what you've done by checking the boxes on the Keeping Track chart found in the Table of Contents.

What do I do when I finish a lesson?

Take the test that goes with that lesson. You don't have to take the test right after you finish the lesson. But if you can, it is a good idea to do one lesson and one test each time you work in your book. To do that, you'll need to plan on one hour of study time. Sometimes, you will finish a lesson and a test in 30 minutes. Other times, you will need the entire hour.

What should I do when I finish a test?

Check your answers and record your score just like you did for the Tryout Test.

What do I do when I finish all the lessons and tests in one part of the book?

Take Tryout Test 2 for that part of the book. Once again, check your answers in the Answer Key and record the number of questions you got correct on the test page and on the Keeping Score chart. Finally, compare your Tryout Test 1 and Tryout Test 2 scores. Then: CELEBRATE!! You are on your way to better test scores and better grades.

Top Ten Test-Taking Tips

Each lesson in this book offers two or more tips that will help you answer the kinds of test questions taught in that lesson. On this page, you will find ten tips that will help you become test-wise, no matter what kind of test you're taking.

1 Work in a quiet, comfortable place where you won't be interrupted by TV or radio, telephones, or talking. Be sure to have plenty of scratch paper and sharp, soft-lead (No. 2) pencils with erasers. You'll also need a bell timer or a clock. When you are ready to begin a test, set the timer, or check the clock, to keep track of the number of minutes the test allows.

2 If you feel nervous before a test, try this: close your eyes and take several slow, deep breaths; spend a few minutes relaxing your mind.

3 When you begin a test, quickly scan all of the questions. This will help you see what the test is about and how many questions you will have to answer.

4 It is important to manage your time while taking a test. Begin by checking the number of questions in the test. Also check the amount of time you have to take the test. Try to complete about half the questions by the time you are about halfway through the total test time.

5 Read all DIRECTIONS through twice. Never begin answering questions before you read the directions.

6 Try to answer ALL the test questions. Do the easy ones first. When you come to a hard question, don't spend a lot of time trying to figure it out. Wait until you have finished all the easy questions, then go back and work on the hard ones.

7 All tests have some hard questions. They are meant to stump you! Don't skip the hard questions. It is much better to guess at the answer. First, find any choices you *know* are wrong. Then look at the leftover choices and make your best guess. Often you will guess right.

8 Mark your answers by filling in the circle with a dark pencil mark. If you make a mistake, erase thoroughly. Then fill in the circle next to the *correct* answer.

9 Stop when you come to the STOP sign at the end of the test, or when your time is up. If you still have time, go back and work on any questions you skipped, or go back and recheck your answers.

10 Remember, we all learn from our mistakes! When your test has been scored, look over the questions you *missed*. Go back and study each one until you know why you missed it. If you still don't understand a question, ask for help.

Reading

Top Ten Reading Tips

1 When asked to answer questions about a reading passage, read the *questions f*irst. That way, you'll know what to look for as you read the passage. When you finish the passage, go on to answer the questions.

2 In reading questions, look for key words, such as *who, what, when, where, why,* and *how,* that tell you what to look for when you read the passage.

3 Practice scanning a reading passage to quickly find key words that will help you answer questions about details.

4 When answering questions about a reading passage, look back at the passage to locate the answer. Don't just rely on your memory.

5 In a reading passage, when you come to a word you don't know, look for context clues: other words in the sentence or paragraph that help to define or explain the unknown word.

6 For fill-in sentences, always read the *entire* sentence before you choose an answer. Use context clues to help you find the answer.

7 When asked to choose a word to complete a sentence, try out all the answer choices in the sentence. Don't rush to fill in the blank; you might get tricked by words that are similar but have different meanings.

8 When looking for word meanings, read all the answer choices carefully. Don't be fooled by words that only *look* or *sound* like the correct answer.

9 When asked to identify order of events, look for key words that signal time sequence, for example: *first, next, then, after, finally,* and *at last.*

10 Watch out for negative words in directions, such as NOT or OPPOSITE. These words tell you exactly what answer to look for. Such words often appear in **bold** or *italic* type, or in ALL CAPITAL LETTERS.

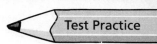

*This test will tell you how well you might score on a standardized reading test **before** using this book.*

Reading Tryout Test 1

Time: **30** minutes

Directions: Follow the directions for each part of the test. Read each question carefully and fill in the circle beside the answer you choose. The answer to the sample question (**S**) has been filled in for you.

Questions 1–14. Look at the key word. One or more letters are underlined. Find the word that has the same sound as the underlined letters.

S ni<u>c</u>e

  Ⓐ pin<u>c</u>h
  ● sent
  Ⓒ cone

1. li<u>st</u>

  Ⓐ stain
  Ⓑ toss
  Ⓒ mask

2. tro<u>ph</u>y

  Ⓐ patch
  Ⓑ hope
  Ⓒ fire

3. pi<u>ll</u>ow

  Ⓐ calm
  Ⓑ leap
  Ⓒ talk

4. pea<u>ch</u>

  Ⓐ cloth
  Ⓑ hush
  Ⓒ chain

5. <u>s</u>mall

  Ⓐ smart
  Ⓑ hums
  Ⓒ snap

6. <u>k</u>ing

  Ⓐ know
  Ⓑ cart
  Ⓒ mix

7. <u>j</u>oker

  Ⓐ kernel
  Ⓑ rake
  Ⓒ cage

8. <u>b</u>and

  Ⓐ lane
  Ⓑ barge
  Ⓒ lamb

9. dir<u>ty</u>

  Ⓐ curl
  Ⓑ ripe
  Ⓒ wire

10. tri<u>ed</u>

  Ⓐ belief
  Ⓑ nearby
  Ⓒ forty

11. <u>bear</u>

  Ⓐ heart
  Ⓑ stair
  Ⓒ learn

12. <u>n</u>oise

  Ⓐ toy
  Ⓑ pilot
  Ⓒ snows

13. c<u>oo</u>l

  Ⓐ shook
  Ⓑ loud
  Ⓒ rude

14. op<u>en</u>

  Ⓐ lightly
  Ⓑ folder
  Ⓒ salad

GO ON ⇒

Reading Tryout Test 1 (continued)

Questions 15–18. Find the word or group of words that means the same as the underlined word.

15. To be <u>fortunate</u> is to be —

    Ⓐ friendly   Ⓒ lucky
    Ⓑ careful   Ⓓ upset

16. To <u>display</u> is to —

    Ⓐ show   Ⓒ change
    Ⓑ hide   Ⓓ fix

17. A <u>glimpse</u> is a —

    Ⓐ light tap   Ⓒ small step
    Ⓑ good idea   Ⓓ quick look

18. <u>Numerous</u> means the same as —

    Ⓐ nervous   Ⓒ wealthy
    Ⓑ many   Ⓓ hidden

Questions 19–20. Find the word that means the OPPOSITE of the underlined word.

19. always <u>doubt</u>

    Ⓐ help   Ⓒ return
    Ⓑ believe   Ⓓ pretend

20. <u>construct</u> quickly

    Ⓐ build   Ⓒ speak
    Ⓑ erect   Ⓓ destroy

Questions 21–22. Find the word that means the same as the underlined word in the sentence.

21. The <u>obstinate</u> mule refused to move. <u>Obstinate</u> means —

    Ⓐ tired   Ⓒ hungry
    Ⓑ stubborn   Ⓓ gentle

22. Jed <u>seized</u> the ball before I could pass it. <u>Seized</u> means —

    Ⓐ grabbed   Ⓒ kicked
    Ⓑ shook   Ⓓ caught

Questions 23–24. Read the sentence in the box. Then find the sentence in which the underlined word has the same meaning.

23. | I can't <u>stand</u> cold weather. |

    Ⓐ Don't <u>stand</u> in my way.
    Ⓑ <u>Stand</u> against the wall.
    Ⓒ Can you <u>stand</u> this music?
    Ⓓ The fruit <u>stand</u> is open.

24. | It was a <u>fair</u> decision. |

    Ⓐ Can we go to the <u>fair</u>?
    Ⓑ The <u>fair</u> princess sleeps.
    Ⓒ The state <u>fair</u> is next week.
    Ⓓ I don't think this law is <u>fair</u>.

GO ON

Questions 25–36. Read each passage. Choose the best answer to each question.

Did your alarm clock shriek at you this morning? Have you ever wanted to throw your alarm clock out the window? Well, you can blame Levi Hutchins for waking you up every day.

In 1787, Levi Hutchins made the first alarm clock. Although Hutchins's alarm clock was large, it was simple to use and it worked well. Over the years, other kinds of alarms have been invented. The E-Z Wake clock was made in 1888, but it did not last long. This strange clock worked by dropping an object on the sleeping person's head.

Later on, the Alarm-O-Bed was invented. When it was time to wake up, this alarm tossed the sleeping person out of bed. Not long ago, someone made a device that wakes a sleeper with an electric shock. It's not surprising that simple alarm clocks, which ring or play radio music, are more widely used than this device. And, when you think about it, maybe Levi Hutchins's first alarm clock wasn't so bad after all.

25. According to this passage, what happened first?

Ⓐ The E-Z Wake clock was invented.

Ⓑ Levi Hutchins made a simple alarm clock.

Ⓒ Someone invented a clock that shocks the sleeper.

Ⓓ Alarm clocks began to play radio music.

26. People usually buy alarm clocks because they —

Ⓐ need help waking up

Ⓑ like fancy devices

Ⓒ don't wear watches

Ⓓ are not good inventors

27. The Alarm-O-Bed woke up a sleeper by —

Ⓐ dropping an object on the person's head

Ⓑ giving the person a shock

Ⓒ playing radio music

Ⓓ tossing the person on the floor

28. From reading this passage, you know that —

Ⓐ most people don't need to use alarm clocks

Ⓑ some people like to think of new inventions

Ⓒ an electric shock won't wake up most people

Ⓓ clocks that play music are hard to use

11

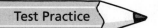

Reading Tryout Test 1 (continued)

On a warm summer day, Pam and Max rowed their little boat out to the middle of the lake. Then they picked up their fishing poles, put some bait on the hooks, and cast their lines into the water. For a long time nothing happened. Then Pam felt a tug on her fishing pole.

"I think I've got a big fish," she said.

"That's great," answered Max. "Hold on and reel it in."

As Max spoke, something strange happened. The boat lurched forward and started speeding toward the shore.

"The fish is pulling us along behind it!" shouted Pam.

"Drop your pole before we crash into the shore!" exclaimed Max. Pam let go of her fishing pole. As it sank into the water, the boat slowed to a stop. Pam and Max sighed with relief. Then they heard a splashing sound. They turned and saw a goldfish the size of an elephant leaping out of the water. It flapped its fins for a second, then disappeared into the lake.

Max and Pam looked at the water for a minute. Then Max said, "Let's keep this story to ourselves. No one would believe us anyway."

29. Where were Pam and Max fishing?

Ⓐ on the ocean

Ⓑ in a river

Ⓒ on a lake

Ⓓ in a brook

30. Why did the boat lurch forward?

Ⓐ Max was rowing it.

Ⓑ The fish was pulling it.

Ⓒ Pam stood up in the boat.

Ⓓ The fish bumped into it.

31. When Pam and Max saw the fish, they were probably —

Ⓐ amazed

Ⓑ embarrassed

Ⓒ angry

Ⓓ calm

32. Which sentence tells something that could NOT really happen?

Ⓐ Pam and Max went fishing.

Ⓑ Pam felt a tug on her line.

Ⓒ The goldfish was the size of an elephant.

Ⓓ The goldfish had fins.

GO ON

Many wild birds depend on people for their food. This is especially true in places where many houses and roads have been built. When people build, they take over open land where birds look for food. Then if people don't provide food for them, the birds must find a new place to live.

There are many ways to feed birds. One way is to put up bird feeders filled with seed. Blackbirds and cardinals like to eat from feeders. Other birds, such as sparrows, like to eat seeds that are scattered on the ground. Robins enjoy eating pieces of apples and oranges. Planting fruit trees is an even better way to attract birds that have a sweet tooth. If your yard has an oak tree, crows and woodpeckers may pay you a visit. A simple flower garden will attract the beautiful hummingbird.

You can try one of these ideas, or all of them. Don't worry if you don't see any birds at first. It may take a while for them to find the food. Once they find it, though, they'll keep coming back for more.

33. This passage is mostly about —

Ⓐ building on open land

Ⓑ planting trees

Ⓒ feeding wild birds

Ⓓ finding seeds

34. A bird that has a <u>sweet tooth</u> is a bird that —

Ⓐ sings a sweet song

Ⓑ has a row of tiny teeth

Ⓒ has bright colors

Ⓓ likes food that is sweet

35. How are blackbirds and cardinals alike?

Ⓐ They eat from feeders.

Ⓑ They live in oak trees.

Ⓒ They look for apples.

Ⓓ They like flower gardens.

36. Which sentence is an <u>opinion</u>?

Ⓐ Many birds depend on people for food.

Ⓑ Sparrows like to eat seeds.

Ⓒ There are many ways to feed birds.

Ⓓ Hummingbirds are beautiful.

Number Correct/Total = _____ /36

Consonant Sounds

Recognizing consonant sounds and letters

Directions: Look at the key word. One or more letters are underlined. Find the word that has the same sound as the underlined letters.

A st̲uck

Ⓐ rack
Ⓑ tusk
Ⓒ waste

B c̲h̲in

Ⓐ beach
Ⓑ shin
Ⓒ clean

This kind of question tests how well you know sounds and letters. In Example A, the key word is *stuck*. The underlined letters are *st*. The only answer choice that has the *st* sound is answer Ⓒ, *waste*.

In Example B, *ch* is underlined. The only word that has the *ch* sound is *beach*, answer Ⓐ.

Hints

Each consonant sound may have one, two, or three letters. It may be in the beginning, in the middle, or at the end of a word. Here are some of the more difficult consonant sounds and different ways to spell them. Say each word and listen to the sounds of the **bold** letters.

Sounds	Spellings
f	**f**ind, of**f**er, **ph**one, rou**gh**
j	**j**am, **g**em, e**dg**e
k	**c**ome, ta**k**e, ro**ck**
m	ti**m**e, su**mm**er, cli**mb**, colu**mn**
n	**n**ow, di**nn**er, **kn**ee, **gn**aw
r	**r**ide, a**rr**ow, **wr**ite
s	**s**eed, mi**ss**, de**c**ide, **sc**ene
t	**t**op, be**tt**er, li**ght**, miss**ed**

Test-Taking Tips

1 Say each word to yourself so you can hear the sounds.

2 Watch out for words that look almost the same, but do not have the same sound, as in *chin* and *shin*.

3 Don't be fooled by different spellings of the same sound, as in **f**ind and **ph**one. Remember, you are listening for the same sound, not looking for the same spelling.

Go for it

Test Practice 1: Consonant Sounds
Time: **8** minutes

Directions: Look at the key word. One or more letters are underlined.
Find the word that has the same sound as the underlined letters.

1. race
    - Ⓐ dress
    - Ⓑ back
    - Ⓒ chirp

2. share
    - Ⓐ peach
    - Ⓑ ashes
    - Ⓒ disk

3. moth
    - Ⓐ think
    - Ⓑ ought
    - Ⓒ their

4. knot
    - Ⓐ chest
    - Ⓑ king
    - Ⓒ manner

5. bright
    - Ⓐ hug
    - Ⓑ late
    - Ⓒ though

6. gentle
    - Ⓐ wiggle
    - Ⓑ jelly
    - Ⓒ ground

7. photo
    - Ⓐ hope
    - Ⓑ cliff
    - Ⓒ path

8. drink
    - Ⓐ jungle
    - Ⓑ snack
    - Ⓒ ankle

9. tiger
    - Ⓐ with
    - Ⓑ passed
    - Ⓒ then

10. fuzzy
    - Ⓐ raise
    - Ⓑ scene
    - Ⓒ lock

11. colt
    - Ⓐ flat
    - Ⓑ built
    - Ⓒ talked

12. lamb
    - Ⓐ elbow
    - Ⓑ band
    - Ⓒ autumn

13. wrong
    - Ⓐ repeat
    - Ⓑ white
    - Ⓒ pillow

14. strap
    - Ⓐ instruct
    - Ⓑ trusted
    - Ⓒ stirring

15. twinkle
    - Ⓐ two
    - Ⓑ between
    - Ⓒ towed

Number Correct/Total = _____ /15

Vowel Sounds

Recognizing vowel sounds and letters

Directions: Look at the key word. One or more letters are underlined. Find the word that has the same vowel sound as the underlined letters.

A team

    Ⓐ keep

    Ⓑ lend

    Ⓒ germ

B crack

    Ⓐ same

    Ⓑ barn

    Ⓒ pass

In Example A, the underlined *ea* is the long *e* sound. The only answer choice that has the long *e* sound is *keep*, answer Ⓐ. In Example B, the underlined letter is the short *a* sound, as in *pass*, answer Ⓒ.

Hints

Each sound may have one or two vowels. It may be in the beginning, in the middle, or at the end of a word. Here are some of the vowel sounds and different ways to spell them. As you say each word aloud, listen carefully for the sound of the vowel (in **bold** letters).

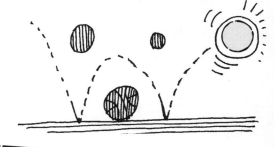

Sounds	Spellings
Short vowel sounds:	**a**dd, r**e**d, h**i**t, r**o**ck, b**u**mp, g**y**m
Long vowel sounds:	l**a**te, r**ai**n, f**ee**t, m**ea**t, **i**ce, r**o**pe, s**oa**p, c**u**te, tr**y**
Vowels followed by *r*:	c**ar**, c**ar**e, **ear**th, h**ear**t, t**er**m, b**ir**d, c**or**n, w**or**d, h**ur**t, c**ur**e
Special vowel sounds:	h**au**l, p**aw**, t**oo**k, m**oo**n, t**oy**, b**oi**l, **ou**t, c**ow**

Test-Taking Tips

1 Say each word to yourself so you can hear the sounds.

2 Look out for answer choices that are spelled differently but have the same vowel sound, as in t**ea**m and k**ee**p.

Go for i

Test Practice 2: Vowel Sounds

Time: 8 minutes

Directions: Look at the key word. One or more letters are underlined. Find the word that has the same vowel sound as the underlined letters.

1. burn
   - Ⓐ through
   - Ⓑ perch
   - Ⓒ crumb

2. tent
   - Ⓐ week
   - Ⓑ they
   - Ⓒ head

3. pail
   - Ⓐ waste
   - Ⓑ certain
   - Ⓒ half

4. still
   - Ⓐ twirl
   - Ⓑ mile
   - Ⓒ crisp

5. flower
   - Ⓐ cloud
   - Ⓑ grow
   - Ⓒ bought

6. season
   - Ⓐ neither
   - Ⓑ break
   - Ⓒ escape

7. bone
   - Ⓐ monkey
   - Ⓑ window
   - Ⓒ should

8. myself
   - Ⓐ baby
   - Ⓑ time
   - Ⓒ key

9. lemon
   - Ⓐ item
   - Ⓑ unfold
   - Ⓒ below

10. mark
    - Ⓐ trap
    - Ⓑ part
    - Ⓒ learn

11. coin
    - Ⓐ powder
    - Ⓑ royal
    - Ⓒ smooth

12. caught
    - Ⓐ laugh
    - Ⓑ dare
    - Ⓒ claw

13. noon
    - Ⓐ cook
    - Ⓑ soup
    - Ⓒ mouth

14. buddy
    - Ⓐ house
    - Ⓑ tube
    - Ⓒ jump

15. three
    - Ⓐ been
    - Ⓑ story
    - Ⓒ wearing

Number Correct/Total = _____ /15

Prefixes, Suffixes, and Root Words

Recognizing prefixes, suffixes, and root words

Directions: Read the key word. Choose the answer that is the root word.

A strangest

   Ⓐ ran

   Ⓑ strange

   Ⓒ rang

   Ⓓ range

Directions: Read the key word. Find the words that mean the same as the key word.

B incomplete

   Ⓐ not complete

   Ⓑ become complete

   Ⓒ complete again

   Ⓓ complete before

Example A asks you to find the root, or base, of a word with a prefix, suffix, or ending such as *est* or *ing*. In this kind of question, the root, or base, is close to the meaning of the key word. *Strange* is the only answer choice that is close to the meaning of *strangest*, so Ⓑ is correct.

Example B asks you to find the meaning of the key word. The key word has the prefix *in*, which means "not." The correct answer is Ⓐ, *not complete*.

Hints

A **prefix** is a word part added to the beginning of a word. A **suffix** or other **word ending(s)** may be added to the end of a word.

Here are some of the common prefixes, suffixes, and other endings. In each word, draw a line between the root word and the prefix, suffix, or other word ending. Then say the root word aloud.

Prefixes: discolor, incomplete, misprint, preschool, unhappy, reread

Suffixes: careless, magical, action, childish, quickly, washable

Other endings: wishes, burning, walked, hurried, sharper, newest

Test-Taking Tips

1 To find the root word, look for the answer choice that is closest in meaning to the key word, as in *strangest/strange*. It will usually be the longest answer choice.

2 To find the meaning of the key word, first separate the root word from the prefix or suffix. (incomplete = *in* + *complete*) Then look for the meaning of the prefix or suffix in the answer choices.

Go for it

Test Practice 3:
Prefixes, Suffixes, and Root Words

Time: **10** minutes

Questions 1–6. Read the key word. Choose the answer that is the root word.

1. ashes
   - Ⓐ she
   - Ⓑ ash
   - Ⓒ he
   - Ⓓ as

2. discourage
   - Ⓐ courage
   - Ⓑ disc
   - Ⓒ our
   - Ⓓ rage

3. nearest
   - Ⓐ ear
   - Ⓑ rest
   - Ⓒ are
   - Ⓓ near

4. restart
   - Ⓐ rest
   - Ⓑ star
   - Ⓒ start
   - Ⓓ art

5. noticeable
   - Ⓐ not
   - Ⓑ able
   - Ⓒ ice
   - Ⓓ notice

6. covering
   - Ⓐ cover
   - Ⓑ ring
   - Ⓒ cove
   - Ⓓ over

Questions 7–12. Read the key word. Find the words that mean the same as the key word.

7. mistreat
   - Ⓐ treat again
   - Ⓑ treat before
   - Ⓒ treat badly
   - Ⓓ treat well

8. thoughtless
   - Ⓐ without thought
   - Ⓑ filled with thought
   - Ⓒ like a thought
   - Ⓓ able to be thought

9. preplan
   - Ⓐ plan again
   - Ⓑ plan before
   - Ⓒ plan well
   - Ⓓ plan after

10. hopeful
    - Ⓐ without hope
    - Ⓑ hope before
    - Ⓒ filled with hope
    - Ⓓ hope again

11. disapprove
    - Ⓐ not approve
    - Ⓑ approve quickly
    - Ⓒ able to approve
    - Ⓓ approve before

12. rapidly
    - Ⓐ somewhat rapid
    - Ⓑ not rapid
    - Ⓒ too rapid
    - Ⓓ in a rapid way

Number Correct/Total = _____ /12

19

Compound Words and Contractions

Recognizing compound words and contractions

class

room

classroom

Directions: Choose the compound word.

A Ⓐ showtime
   Ⓑ interesting
   Ⓒ preview
   Ⓓ frequent

Directions: Read the contraction. Find the phrase that means the same as the contraction.

B wasn't

   Ⓐ would not
   Ⓑ were not
   Ⓒ was not
   Ⓓ will not

Example A asks you to find the compound word. A **compound word** is made up of two smaller words. The correct answer is Ⓐ, *showtime*. It is made up of two smaller words, *show* and *time*.

Example B asks you to find the phrase that means the same as the contraction *wasn't*. A **contraction** is formed by taking out part of a word and putting in an apostrophe ('). The correct answer is Ⓒ, *was not*. This means the same as *wasn't*. The apostrophe in *wasn't* replaces the letter *o* in *not*.

Hints

Practice looking for the parts of a compound word. Draw a line between the two words in each compound word below. Then think of some other compound words you know.

nighttime	airplane	classroom
bathtub	grasshopper	evergreen

A contraction is a way of combining two words. Here are some common contractions and their meanings. Cross out the letter or letters that have been replaced by an apostrophe.

don't	do not	**aren't**	are not
I'm	I am	**she's**	she is
they've	they have	**you're**	you are

Test-Taking Tips

1 To find a compound word, look for the word that has two smaller words which can stand alone.

2 To find the meaning of a contraction, look for the phrase that is spelled most like the contraction.

Go for it

Test Practice 4:
Compound Words and Contractions

Time: **10** minutes

Questions 1–8. Choose the compound word.

---

1. Ⓐ barefoot
   Ⓑ finished
   Ⓒ amusement
   Ⓓ excellent

2. Ⓐ nonsense
   Ⓑ birthday
   Ⓒ envelope
   Ⓓ narrower

3. Ⓐ decorate
   Ⓑ wonderful
   Ⓒ faraway
   Ⓓ countries

4. Ⓐ caterpillar
   Ⓑ underground
   Ⓒ goodness
   Ⓓ unwelcome

5. Ⓐ accident
   Ⓑ fearful
   Ⓒ sweetest
   Ⓓ toothbrush

6. Ⓐ emperor
   Ⓑ invention
   Ⓒ whenever
   Ⓓ looking

7. Ⓐ refurnish
   Ⓑ monument
   Ⓒ princesses
   Ⓓ newspaper

8. Ⓐ campfire
   Ⓑ sentence
   Ⓒ fluttered
   Ⓓ assistant

Questions 9–14. Find the phrase that means the same as the contraction.

---

9. won't
   Ⓐ will not
   Ⓑ was not
   Ⓒ were not
   Ⓓ would not

10. they're
    Ⓐ they will
    Ⓑ they have
    Ⓒ they are
    Ⓓ they had

11. you've
    Ⓐ you will
    Ⓑ you are
    Ⓒ you give
    Ⓓ you have

12. it's
    Ⓐ it should
    Ⓑ it shall
    Ⓒ it is
    Ⓓ it does

13. couldn't
    Ⓐ can not
    Ⓑ could have
    Ⓒ can it
    Ⓓ could not

14. she'll
    Ⓐ she will
    Ⓑ she has
    Ⓒ she would
    Ⓓ she had

STOP

Number Correct/Total = _____ /14

21

Word Meaning

Identifying the meaning of words

Directions: Choose the word or words that have the same meaning as the underlined word.

A A <u>noise</u> is a —

   Ⓐ sound

   Ⓑ book

   Ⓒ listener

   Ⓓ smell

B To <u>guide</u> is to —

   Ⓐ guard

   Ⓑ lead

   Ⓒ follow

   Ⓓ glide

In Example A, the underlined word is *noise*. A noise is a kind of *sound*, so the correct answer is Ⓐ. None of the other choices fits. In Example B, the word *guide* means to *lead*, so the correct answer is Ⓑ.

Hint

You can improve your vocabulary by reading a book or magazine that is just a little bit difficult for you. When you see a word you don't know, write the word down in a notebook. Then look up the word in the dictionary and write its meaning in your notebook.

Here is a sentence to get you started. Write down any words you don't know and look them up in a dictionary.

The helicopter hovered for a moment above the canyon, then sped off toward the mesa.

Test-Taking Tips

1 Think about what the underlined word means before you look at the answers.

2 Watch out for answers that are closely related to the key word, but do not have the same meaning. In Example A, *listener* is closely related to *noise*, but it does not have the same meaning.

3 Watch out for sound-alike words, look-alike words, and opposites. In Example B, *guard* is a sound-alike word; *follow* is an opposite; and *glide* is a look-alike word.

Go for it

Test Practice 5 : Word Meaning

Time: **10** minutes

Directions: Choose the word or words that have the same meaning as the underlined word.

1. A <u>parcel</u> is a —

   (A) package   (C) chore

   (B) coat   (D) gift

2. To <u>descend</u> is to —

   (A) count on   (C) go down

   (B) look for   (D) throw out

3. To be <u>exhausted</u> is to be —

   (A) too small   (C) almost done

   (B) very tired   (D) far away

4. A <u>lullaby</u> is a —

   (A) story   (C) problem

   (B) riddle   (D) song

5. <u>Slender</u> means the same as —

   (A) light   (C) small

   (B) thin   (D) smooth

6. A <u>pebble</u> is a —

   (A) dark spot   (C) shiny coin

   (B) cold place   (D) tiny stone

7. <u>Swiftly</u> means the same as —

   (A) quickly   (C) neatly

   (B) kindly   (D) gracefully

8. To be <u>cautious</u> is to be —

   (A) lucky   (C) bossy

   (B) early   (D) careful

9. Something that is <u>amusing</u> is —

   (A) boring   (C) funny

   (B) harmful   (D) strange

10. Something that is <u>filthy</u> is —

    (A) large   (C) deep

    (B) clever   (D) dirty

11. A <u>nuisance</u> is —

    (A) a bother   (C) a mistake

    (B) a surprise   (D) an errand

12. To <u>assemble</u> is to —

    (A) look like   (C) speak to

    (B) put together   (D) go away

Number Correct/Total = _____ /12

23

Synonyms and Antonyms

Recognizing synonyms and antonyms

Directions: Find the word that means the same, or almost the same, as the underlined word.

A birthday <u>present</u>

   Ⓐ surprise

   Ⓑ party

   Ⓒ gift

   Ⓓ award

Directions: Find the word that means the OPPOSITE of the underlined word.

B <u>tame</u> animal

   Ⓐ wild

   Ⓑ gentle

   Ⓒ strange

   Ⓓ huge

Words that have the same, or almost the same, meaning are **synonyms.** In Example A, *gift*, choice Ⓒ, is a synonym for *present*. The other answer choices may be related to *birthday* or *present*, but none of them means the same as *present*.

Words that have opposite meanings are **antonyms.** In Example B, the antonym for *tame* is *wild,* choice Ⓐ. All of the choices may describe animals, but only one means the opposite of *tame*.

Test-Taking Tips

1 When looking for synonyms, watch out for answer choices that are closely related but do not have the same meaning — and watch out for opposites. (In Example A, *surprise* and *party* seem to be related, but neither choice means the same as *present*.)

2 When looking for antonyms, look for words that have opposite meanings. Watch out for choices that actually mean the same. (In Example B, choice Ⓑ, *gentle*, means the same as *tame*.)

Go for it

Test Practice 6: Synonyms and Antonyms   Time: 8 minutes

Questions 1–5. Find the word that means the same, or almost the same, as the underlined word.

Questions 6–10. Find the word that means the OPPOSITE of the underlined word.

1. <u>cruel</u> trick
   - Ⓐ clever
   - Ⓑ mean
   - Ⓒ unusual
   - Ⓓ daring

2. suddenly <u>disappear</u>
   - Ⓐ vanish
   - Ⓑ return
   - Ⓒ stop
   - Ⓓ remember

3. <u>sincere</u> answer
   - Ⓐ best
   - Ⓑ surprising
   - Ⓒ truthful
   - Ⓓ foolish

4. don't <u>fret</u>
   - Ⓐ leave
   - Ⓑ forget
   - Ⓒ try
   - Ⓓ worry

5. kept <u>squirming</u>
   - Ⓐ wiggling
   - Ⓑ looking
   - Ⓒ laughing
   - Ⓓ sleeping

6. <u>lend</u> money
   - Ⓐ spend
   - Ⓑ borrow
   - Ⓒ count
   - Ⓓ give

7. is <u>healthy</u>
   - Ⓐ poor
   - Ⓑ fair
   - Ⓒ ill
   - Ⓓ strong

8. <u>innocent</u> person
   - Ⓐ strange
   - Ⓑ kind
   - Ⓒ guilty
   - Ⓓ angry

9. became <u>discouraged</u>
   - Ⓐ upset
   - Ⓑ curious
   - Ⓒ interested
   - Ⓓ hopeful

10. can <u>create</u>
    - Ⓐ imagine
    - Ⓑ find
    - Ⓒ destroy
    - Ⓓ direct

Number Correct/Total = _____ /10

Context Clues

Using context clues to find word meanings and to define multiple-meaning words

Directions: Read the sentence. Find the meaning of the underlined word.

A Greg stopped laughing when he saw the <u>grim</u> look on Mom's face. <u>Grim</u> means —

  Ⓐ calm   Ⓒ serious

  Ⓑ silly   Ⓓ amused

Directions: Read the sentence in the box. Then find the sentence in which the underlined word is used in the same way.

B | We sat on the river <u>bank</u>. |

  Ⓐ There was a <u>bank</u> of telephone booths along the wall.

  Ⓑ I have to go to the <u>bank</u> today.

  Ⓒ If you <u>bank</u> the coals, the fire will burn more evenly.

  Ⓓ Pete was fishing from the <u>bank</u>.

These are context clues questions. **Context clues** are the other words in the sentence or sentences that can help you understand word meaning. Context clues can help you understand the meaning of a word you don't know.

In Example A, you are asked to find the meaning of the underlined word *grim*. The sentence suggests that Greg's laughing stopped because he saw the *grim* look on his mother's face. So *grim* must mean something that is not funny. The answer is Ⓒ, *serious*.

Context clues also can suggest the correct meaning of words that have **multiple meanings.** In Example B, the underlined word *bank* has more than one meaning. You must figure out what *bank* means in the first sentence, then find another sentence in which it means the same thing. The sentence in the box suggests that the *bank* is the land beside a river. Answer Ⓓ, "Pete was fishing from the bank," uses the word in the same way. The other sentences use other meanings of the word *bank*.

Test-Taking Tips

1 Read the whole sentence carefully. Decide what the underlined word means in the key sentence before you look at the answer choices.

2 For unfamiliar words: When you choose an answer, try it out in the original sentence to see if it makes sense. ("Greg stopped laughing when he saw the *serious* look on his mother's face.")

3 For multiple-meaning words: Think of all the different meanings you know for the underlined word, then choose the one that is used in the key sentence.

Go

Test Practice 7: Context Clues

Time: **8** minutes

Questions 1–5. Read the sentence. Find the meaning of the underlined word.

1. This factory <u>manufactures</u> tires for cars, trucks, and bicycles. <u>Manufactures</u> means —

   Ⓐ makes   Ⓒ uses

   Ⓑ saves   Ⓓ grows

2. Although Rita is just a <u>novice</u>, she is already becoming a good skier. <u>Novice</u> means —

   Ⓐ athlete   Ⓒ beginner

   Ⓑ friend   Ⓓ instructor

3. The child <u>harassed</u> the dog by pulling its tail. <u>Harassed</u> means —

   Ⓐ petted   Ⓒ trained

   Ⓑ bothered   Ⓓ ignored

4. The clown's <u>comical</u> costume made the audience laugh. <u>Comical</u> means —

   Ⓐ new   Ⓒ fancy

   Ⓑ neat   Ⓓ funny

5. Jake is an <u>easygoing</u> person who doesn't let anything upset him. <u>Easygoing</u> means —

   Ⓐ relaxed   Ⓒ serious

   Ⓑ hardworking   Ⓓ popular

Questions 6–10. Read the sentence in the box. Find the sentence in which the underlined word is used in the same way.

6. | Wash your hands and <u>face</u>. |

   Ⓐ Stand and <u>face</u> the wall.

   Ⓑ Place the card <u>face</u> down.

   Ⓒ A tear ran down his <u>face</u>.

   Ⓓ We must <u>face</u> the truth.

7. | The clay is dry and <u>hard</u>. |

   Ⓐ Pull <u>hard</u> on the handle.

   Ⓑ This is a <u>hard</u> puzzle.

   Ⓒ They worked <u>hard</u> today.

   Ⓓ We sat on the <u>hard</u> floor.

8. | Do you <u>mind</u> if we watch? |

   Ⓐ I <u>mind</u> the cold weather.

   Ⓑ Bill's <u>mind</u> is made up.

   Ⓒ Please <u>mind</u> your manners.

   Ⓓ Joan has a creative <u>mind</u>.

9. | How did the radio <u>break</u>? |

   Ⓐ Let's take a <u>break</u> now.

   Ⓑ <u>Break</u> a twig off the tree.

   Ⓒ The storm will <u>break</u> soon.

   Ⓓ The glasses <u>break</u> easily.

10. | Don't <u>press</u> the red button! |

    Ⓐ Did you <u>press</u> my pants?

    Ⓑ <u>Press</u> down on this lever.

    Ⓒ The <u>press</u> is waiting outside.

    Ⓓ The crowd began to <u>press</u> forward.

 STOP

Number Correct/Total = _____ /10

Main Idea and Details

Finding the main idea and supporting details in a reading passage

Directions: Read the passage. Choose the best answer to each question.

Jack and the Beanstalk is a fairy tale about a boy and a giant. There are also many folk tales and legends about giants. The idea of giants probably started long ago with the Greeks. The Greeks believed that their ancestors were very tall and strong. They thought that people had become smaller and weaker as time went on. The Greeks told many stories about giants. In these stories, the giants stood for the forces of nature, such as earth, water, and air. The Greeks' giant stories spread to other parts of the world. Soon people from other lands made up their own stories about giants.

A What is the best title for this passage?

   Ⓐ "Jack and the Beanstalk"

   Ⓑ "Greek Stories About Giants"

   Ⓒ "Giants from Many Lands"

   Ⓓ "Folk Tales and Legends"

B What is the main idea of this passage?

   Ⓐ The idea of giants started long ago with the Greeks.

   Ⓑ People become smaller and weaker as time goes on.

   Ⓒ Giants are tall people with great strength.

   Ⓓ People from many lands make up their own stories.

C The Greeks of long ago believed that their ancestors —

   Ⓐ were afraid of nature

   Ⓑ came from other lands

   Ⓒ were tall and strong

   Ⓓ created many legends

D *Jack and the Beanstalk* is a —

   Ⓐ legend

   Ⓑ folk tale

   Ⓒ poem

   Ⓓ fairy tale

Questions about the **main idea and details** may ask you to choose the best title, the main idea, or the main topic of a passage. To answer these questions, you have to decide what the passage is mostly about.

The passage you just read is mostly about how the Greeks created the idea of giants. Example A asks for the best title. Choice Ⓑ, "Greek Stories About Giants," is the only title that describes the **main idea**, that tells what the whole passage is about. The other choices are titles that tell only about details from the passage, not about the main idea.

Example B asks for the main idea of the passage. Choice Ⓐ is the only sentence that describes the main idea. It is also the third sentence in the passage. (In some cases, the main idea will not appear in one sentence from the passage. You will have to choose the answer that best states the main idea, even though it is not taken directly from the passage.)

Questions A and B ask about the main idea. Other questions may ask about **details** that support the main idea. Example C is this type of question. The information you need to answer this question is in the passage. The fourth sentence of the passage tells you what the Greeks believed about their ancestors. Choice Ⓒ is correct.

Other questions may ask about factual details from the passage, as in Example D. You can find the answer to this question in the first sentence of the passage. Choice Ⓓ is correct because the passage says that *Jack and the Beanstalk* is a fairy tale.

Hint

Main ideas and details are important in all kinds of writing. You can practice finding main ideas by reading newspapers, books, magazines — just about anything! Study one paragraph at a time and see if you can find the main idea. Then look for the main idea of the whole passage or article.

Test-Taking Tips

1 Read the whole passage carefully. As you read, try to decide what the passage is mostly about. Sometimes a passage contains one main idea sentence. Sometimes the main idea comes from two or more sentences.

2 If you don't know the answer to a question right away, go back to the passage to find the information you need.

Go for it

Test Practice 8: Main Idea and Details   Time: 10 minutes

Questions 1–8. Read each passage. Choose the best answer to each question.

A plant seed contains a small amount of food. As a plant grows, it uses up the food in the seed. Then the plant needs to take its food from the soil around it. If there is no soil, the plant will die. You can prove this with a simple experiment.

You will need two bowls, a paper napkin, soil, grass seed, and some plastic wrap. Put soil in one bowl. Roll the napkin into a ball and place it inside the other bowl. Sprinkle grass seed into each bowl. Water both bowls lightly. Then cover them with plastic and place them in the sun. After a few days, grass will sprout in each bowl. Remove the plastic wrap from the bowls. Water the grass every day.

What happens? You will see that the grass keeps growing in both bowls for a while. Then the grass in the bowl with the paper napkin will stop growing. The grass will keep growing in the bowl with the soil. Do you know why?

1. What is the main idea of this passage?

    Ⓐ Experiments are fun to do.
    Ⓑ Grass grows from seeds.
    Ⓒ Plants need soil to grow.
    Ⓓ Some plants grow quickly.

2. What finally happens to the grass planted in the bowl with the paper napkin?

    Ⓐ It gets very tall.
    Ⓑ Flowers start to bloom.
    Ⓒ It stops growing.
    Ⓓ The roots grow deep.

3. When you do this experiment, you should cover each bowl with —

    Ⓐ a napkin
    Ⓑ plastic wrap
    Ⓒ a towel
    Ⓓ tin foil

4. What is the best title for this passage?

    Ⓐ How to Plant a Garden
    Ⓑ Experimenting with Bowls
    Ⓒ Growing Grass Inside
    Ⓓ What Seeds Need to Grow

GO ON

The New England Aquarium is a kind of zoo for ocean animals. The Aquarium also cares for hurt or lost ocean animals. One morning an Aquarium worker named Greg Early received some bad news. Forty whales were stranded on a Massachusetts beach.

Greg went to see what could be done for the whales. Healthy adult whales were guided back to the deep ocean waters. Hurt or sick whales had to be put to sleep. Three young whales were a special problem. They had become separated from their mothers and were too young to care for themselves in the ocean. Greg decided to bring the young whales back to the Aquarium.

For six months Greg and his crew cared for the young whales. When the whales were healthy and strong, Greg knew it was time to return them to the ocean. Still, he worried. Would the whales become frightened or lost when they were released? Greg decided to put radio tags on the whales to keep track of them in the ocean. The radio signals would let the crew know if the whales were in trouble.

The young whales were brought to a part of the ocean where a group of whales had been spotted. Greg didn't need to worry after all. When they were released, the three young whales swam away and joined the group.

5. What is this passage mostly about?

   Ⓐ what people can see at the New England Aquarium

   Ⓑ why whales become stranded

   Ⓒ how Greg Early worked to save three young whales

   Ⓓ why whales swim in groups

6. What did Greg decide to do when he saw the three young whales?

   Ⓐ look for their mothers

   Ⓑ guide them to deep water

   Ⓒ put them to sleep

   Ⓓ bring them to the Aquarium

7. How long did Greg Early and his crew care for the whales?

   Ⓐ two months

   Ⓑ four months

   Ⓒ six months

   Ⓓ eight months

8. What is the best title for this passage?

   Ⓐ Working at the New England Aquarium

   Ⓑ The Whale Rescue

   Ⓒ Learning About Ocean Animals

   Ⓓ A Massachusetts Beach

Number Correct/Total = _____ /8

Constructing Meaning

Relating ideas to interpret a reading passage

Directions: Read the passage. Choose the best answer to each question.

As Curtis walked out of the pet store, he held a tiny black kitten in his arms. "I think I'll call her Eve," Curtis said to his mother, "because she's as dark as the evening sky."

When Curtis got home, he set out bowls of food and water for Eve. The kitten tasted the food and began to purr loudly. Curtis petted Eve gently. "We're going to be good friends," he said.

Curtis had always wanted a cat. Dogs are friendlier than cats, and they can guard the owner's home. But dogs need more attention, and they have to be taken for walks every day. Cats, on the other hand, take care of themselves. They are quieter than dogs, and cleaner, too. Curtis went to sleep that night feeling happy that he finally had a cat of his own.

The next morning, Curtis woke up to find Eve sleeping next to his pillow. He reached over to pet her. Suddenly he started to sneeze. His eyes began to water, too. Then as Curtis got dressed, he noticed a red rash on his skin.

Curtis's mother took him to the doctor right away. Dr. Leo examined Curtis carefully. Then she said, "Your mother tells me that you have a new kitten. Some people get sick when they are around cats. I'm afraid that you are one of those people. If you keep your kitten, you will start to feel even worse."

A Which event happens first?

Ⓐ Curtis goes to the doctor.

Ⓑ Curtis goes to bed.

Ⓒ Curtis begins to sneeze.

Ⓓ Curtis feeds the kitten.

B Curtis named the kitten Eve because she —

Ⓐ made him sneeze

Ⓑ was as dark as the evening sky

Ⓒ liked to purr

Ⓓ had an even number of stripes

C How did Curtis probably feel when he heard the news from Dr. Leo?

Ⓐ hopeful

Ⓑ ashamed

Ⓒ proud

Ⓓ unhappy

D Compared with dogs, cats are —

Ⓐ friendlier

Ⓑ noisier

Ⓒ cleaner

Ⓓ more useful

In every passage that you read, ideas are related to one another in certain ways. Some ideas are related by **sequence**, or time order. Example A asks which event happens first in the story, and it lists four things that happen. The first thing Curtis does in this story is come out of the pet shop. Then he names the kitten. Then he feeds the kitten. Of the four events listed in Example A, choice Ⓓ, "Curtis feeds the kitten," is correct.

Some ideas are related by **cause and effect**. Example B asks why Curtis named the kitten Eve. The first paragraph says that he decided to call her Eve "*because* she's as dark as the evening sky." The kitten's dark color is the cause; the name Eve is the effect. So answer Ⓑ is correct.

Some passages just give you different ideas. You have to decide what they mean, or how they are related. This is called **drawing conclusions**. Example C asks how Curtis probably felt when he heard the news from Dr. Leo. The passage tells you that he has always wanted a cat. Curtis tells Eve that "we're going to be good friends." These ideas suggest that Curtis really likes his new pet. When he hears the news from Dr. Leo, he knows that he will have to give away his kitten. He probably feels quite unhappy. So answer Ⓓ is correct.

Some passages **compare and contrast** two or more things by telling how they are alike and how they are different. Example D is about comparing cats and dogs. The third paragraph of the passage says that cats are "quieter than dogs, and cleaner, too." So, answer Ⓒ, *cleaner* (than dogs), is correct. The passage does not say that cats are friendlier, noisier, or more useful than dogs.

Test-Taking Tips

1 When you want to find the sequence of events, look for signal words such as *first, then, next, later, finally,* and *last* (as in "The *next* morning, Curtis woke up...").

2 When you want to find causes and effects, look for signal words such as *because, as a result, since,* and *so.* (For example, "I think I'll call her Eve *because* she's as dark as the evening sky.")

3 When you draw conclusions, look for at least two details in the passage to support the answer you choose.

4 When you compare or contrast two or more things, look for signal words such as *like, same, but, unlike, on the other hand,* and *however.* (For example, "*But* dogs need more attention...").

Go for it

Test Practice 9: Constructing Meaning

Time: **10** minutes

Questions 1–10. Read each passage. Then choose the best answer to each question.

In the 1800s, young women were expected to marry and have children. Maria Mitchell had different ideas, though. Like many girls, Maria went to school to learn to read and write. But she also became very interested in math and science. She studied these subjects so eagerly that she soon knew more than her teachers. Maria's father encouraged her interests. He taught her how to use his telescope to look at the stars and planets. Before long, Maria fell in love with the science of astronomy.

After Maria finished school, she worked in a library. But every night she studied the sky through her telescope. In 1847, Maria discovered a comet. Her discovery made her famous. The king of Denmark gave her a gold medal. Better yet, a group of women bought a special telescope for Maria.

In 1865, Vassar College asked Maria to be a teacher there. Once again her father encouraged her, so Maria took the job. Maria was a great teacher. She also helped Vassar become an important center for astronomy.

1. How was Maria different from most young women in the 1800s?

   Ⓐ She planned to get married.
   Ⓑ She was interested in math and science.
   Ⓒ She went to school.
   Ⓓ She enjoyed caring for children.

2. From reading this story, you know that Maria's father —

   Ⓐ was jealous when Maria became famous
   Ⓑ made many discoveries with his telescope
   Ⓒ wanted to be a college teacher
   Ⓓ thought women could do many things that men did

3. Maria became famous because she —

   Ⓐ discovered a comet
   Ⓑ built a special telescope
   Ⓒ received a gold medal
   Ⓓ knew more than her teachers

4. A person who studies astronomy mostly —

   Ⓐ teaches young children
   Ⓑ solves math problems
   Ⓒ writes a lot of books
   Ⓓ learns about outer space

5. What did Maria do last?

   Ⓐ studied math in school
   Ⓑ took a job at Vassar College
   Ⓒ worked in a library
   Ⓓ learned to use a telescope

GO ON

After three long days in the car, Tim was glad when Dad said, "We're finally in North Carolina. We'll be at Uncle Stuart's house soon."

Uncle Stuart was preparing dinner when Tim and his father arrived. "Let's eat and get to bed early," Uncle Stuart said. "Tomorrow, we're going to the beach. You'll see what it's like to swim in the ocean, Tim."

"It can't be much different from swimming in a lake in Minnesota," Tim answered.

The next day, Uncle Stuart drove Tim and Dad to the beach. Tim was surprised to see such big, rolling waves. He didn't say anything to Uncle Stuart, though. Then Uncle Stuart saw Tim wrinkle his nose. "That's the smell of salt and seaweed," he said. "You'll get used to it."

Tim pulled off his shirt and shouted, "Well, here I go!" He ran down to the water and jumped in. He was glad the ocean wasn't too cold. It was as warm as the lake in Minnesota. Tim tried to swim out a little, but he did not get far. Just then, Uncle Stuart appeared by his side. "It's hard to swim out against the waves," he said to Tim.

"Oh, it's not so tough," Tim insisted. Just then a wave curled over his head and his mouth filled with salt water. He coughed and sputtered.

Uncle Stuart laughed. "When you swim in the ocean, you learn to keep your mouth closed," he said.

6. What happened just before Tim jumped into the water?

   Ⓐ Uncle Stuart laughed at him.

   Ⓑ He pulled off his shirt.

   Ⓒ His uncle started swimming.

   Ⓓ He saw the big waves.

7. How was the lake in Minnesota the same as the ocean?

   Ⓐ It tasted salty.

   Ⓑ It had big waves.

   Ⓒ It wasn't too cold.

   Ⓓ It had seaweed in it.

8. Tim wrinkled his nose because —

   Ⓐ he smelled something odd

   Ⓑ his nose itched

   Ⓒ the sun was in his eyes

   Ⓓ he was annoyed

9. From reading this story, you can tell that Tim —

   Ⓐ really doesn't like to swim

   Ⓑ has trouble admitting that he is wrong

   Ⓒ thinks that Uncle Stuart is very smart

   Ⓓ is afraid to try new things

10. From reading this story, you can tell that —

   Ⓐ Minnesota is a long way from North Carolina

   Ⓑ there are many lakes in North Carolina

   Ⓒ Minnesota is larger than North Carolina

   Ⓓ swimming isn't a popular sport in Minnesota

Number Correct/Total = _____ /10

Evaluating Information
Making judgments about what you read

Directions: Read the passage. Choose the best answer to each question.

These days, there are special sneakers for many kinds of sports. Should you really spend your money buying different sneakers for every sport you enjoy? Of course you shouldn't! That's why the people at Shoes For You designed the Everything Sneaker. This amazing sneaker supports your feet when you're walking, running, dancing, or jumping. You'll never buy a more comfortable sneaker, either. The Everything Sneaker is lined with soft material that shapes itself to your foot. But don't take our word for it. Buy a pair of Everything Sneakers at your local shoe store. Your feet will thank you for taking such good care of them.

A Which sentence tells about something that could NOT really happen?

 Ⓐ The people at Shoes For You designed the Everything Sneaker.

 Ⓑ The Everything Sneaker supports your feet.

 Ⓒ Your feet will thank you for taking such good care of them.

 Ⓓ There are sneakers for many kinds of sports.

B Which sentence is a fact?

 Ⓐ You shouldn't buy different sneakers for every sport.

 Ⓑ The Everything Sneaker is amazing.

 Ⓒ You'll never buy a more comfortable sneaker.

 Ⓓ The Everything Sneaker is lined with soft material.

C The author wrote this passage mainly to —

 Ⓐ explain how sneakers are made

 Ⓑ convince you to buy a pair of Everything Sneakers

 Ⓒ tell about the people at Shoes For You

 Ⓓ convince you to enjoy a lot of sports

D What is the best reason for buying Everything Sneakers?

 Ⓐ They are sold at local shoe stores.

 Ⓑ They can be used for many sports.

 Ⓒ They cost more than other sneakers.

 Ⓓ They are made by people at Shoes For You.

To answer these kinds of questions, you have to think about what you read and make judgments. This is called **evaluating information**.

A question may ask you to decide what is real and what is not. In Example A, you must find the sentence that tells about something that could NOT happen in real life. Choice Ⓒ is correct, because sneakers cannot speak. The other choices tell about things that could really happen.

A question may ask you to choose a sentence from the passage that is a fact or opinion. A **fact** is something that can be proven true. An **opinion** is a belief or feeling. In Example C, the only fact is sentence Ⓓ. You could prove that Everything Sneakers are lined with soft material by looking at the material and touching it. All the other choices are opinions.

Some questions may ask what the author thinks or why the author wrote the passage. Most passages are written for one of these purposes: to entertain, to give information or directions, to persuade, or to describe something. In Example B, the best answer is Ⓑ. This passage is most like an advertisement. The author wrote it mainly to convince, or persuade, people to buy Everything Sneakers.

Some questions may ask you to use the information in the passage to **make decisions**. In Example D, you must choose the best reason to buy Everything Sneakers. Choice Ⓑ, "They can be used for many sports," is the best reason. You would get more use from these sneakers than from other brands. Most sneakers are sold at local stores, so Ⓐ is not a good reason to buy. There is no reason to buy these sneakers just because they cost more, answer Ⓒ, or because they are made by a certain company, answer Ⓓ.

Test-Taking Tips

1 To find a fact, or something that could really happen, look for things that you can prove to be true.

2 To find an opinion, or something that could not really happen, look for things that you cannot prove to be true.

3 As you read the passage, think about what the author is trying to say, and why. Advertisements are written to persuade. Most stories are written to entertain. Text books, how-to books, and many articles are written to teach, to give information, or to describe something.

4 When you have to make a decision, think about all the reasons for and against the decision. Then choose the most important reason to help you make your decision.

Go for it

Test Practice 10 : Evaluating Information

Time: **9** minutes

Questions 1–8. Read each passage. Then choose the best answer to each question.

Once upon a time there lived an old woodcutter and his daughter, Helen. They lived in a tiny house in the woods. Every morning the woodcutter set to work cutting down trees. To pass the time until he returned, Helen went for walks in the woods. She always filled her pockets with treats for the forest animals, who loved and trusted her. Whenever they heard the sound of her footsteps, they ran to greet her.

One day as Helen walked through the woods, she slipped and fell. She hurt her leg badly and could not walk. The animals gathered around Helen. They tried to comfort her, but Helen was upset. "Soon it will be dark, and my father will not know where I am," said Helen. "What shall I do?"

Just then Owl spoke up. "Let us send for Deer. He is strong enough to carry you back to your father's house." The other animals nodded. "That's a very clever suggestion," they all said. Then Goose and Duck flew off to find Deer. He appeared a few minutes later, and knelt beside Helen. The other animals helped Helen climb onto his back.

Helen waved to her friends as Deer carried her away. "I'll be back again when my leg is better," she promised.

1. Which sentence tells about something that could NOT really happen?

   Ⓐ Helen went for walks in the woods.

   Ⓑ The forest animals heard the sound of Helen's footsteps.

   Ⓒ Helen could not walk after she fell.

   Ⓓ Goose and Duck flew off to find Deer.

2. In this story, the author seems to feel that Helen is —

   Ⓐ beautiful and graceful

   Ⓑ kind and gentle

   Ⓒ shy and afraid

   Ⓓ silly and careless

3. Which sentence is an opinion?

   Ⓐ Helen and her father lived in the woods.

   Ⓑ The woodcutter set to work every morning.

   Ⓒ Helen brought treats for the forest animals.

   Ⓓ Owl's suggestion was very clever.

4. Helen was upset mostly because — .

   Ⓐ she hurt her leg badly

   Ⓑ her father would be worried about her

   Ⓒ the woods were full of wild animals

   Ⓓ she was afraid of the dark

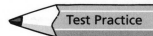

Matt McGee has directed many fine movies, but *Seeing Things* is sure to become his biggest hit. The movie is about a boy named Hal Franklin who makes a surprising discovery. One day Hal mixes up some ingredients in his kitchen. When he spills the mixture on his shoe, his foot disappears! At first Hal is frightened, but after a few minutes his foot appears again. Once Hal knows that the mixture won't hurt him, he makes some more. Then he sets off to cause all kinds of trouble with his magic mixture. Mitch Henry gives a great performance as Hal. Zelda Howe also gets a lot of laughs in her role as Hal's mother. This is a wonderful movie for the whole family, and one you'll remember for years to come. Don't miss it!

5. The author wrote this passage mainly to —

   Ⓐ explain why Matt McGee directs movies

   Ⓑ tell how to make a magic mixture

   Ⓒ persuade people to see the movie *Seeing Things*

   Ⓓ give information about Zelda Howe

6. Which sentence tells about something that could happen in real life?

   Ⓐ Hal mixed some ingredients together.

   Ⓑ The mixture made Hal's foot disappear.

   Ⓒ After a few minutes Hal's foot appeared again.

   Ⓓ Hal caused trouble with his magic mixture.

7. Which sentence is a fact?

   Ⓐ *Seeing Things* is sure to be Matt McGee's biggest hit.

   Ⓑ The movie is about a boy named Hal Franklin.

   Ⓒ Mitch Henry gives a great performance as Hal.

   Ⓓ This is a wonderful movie for the whole family.

8. Which word best describes *Seeing Things*?

   Ⓐ frightening

   Ⓑ serious

   Ⓒ sad

   Ⓓ funny

Number Correct/Total = _____ /8

READING
Lesson 11

Characters and Plot

Understanding the characters and plot in a story

Directions: Read the passage. Choose the best answer to each question.

Mr. Cruz stood at the entrance to the science museum. He held his finger to his lips until his students were quiet. "Boys and girls," he said, "please stay together so that no one gets lost in the museum."

At first Juana didn't have any trouble keeping up with her class. The rock room and the insect room didn't interest her very much. Then Mr. Cruz led the class into the dinosaur room. Juana gasped. One of the dinosaur skeletons was taller than her house! Juana stared at the skeleton for a long time. She had never seen anything like this before. Then she asked, "Mr. Cruz, what ever happened to the dinosaurs?"

No one answered. Juana looked around and realized that her class was gone. "Now I'm lost," she said to herself, wondering what she would do next. But just then, she noticed a friendly-looking museum guard standing by the doorway.

A Mr. Cruz held his finger to his lips to show the class that they should —

  ⓐ quiet down

  ⓑ stay together

  ⓒ follow him

  ⓓ ask questions

B Juana followed her class until they left the —

  ⓐ museum entrance

  ⓑ rock room

  ⓒ dinosaur room

  ⓓ insect room

C When Juana saw the huge skeleton, she felt —

  ⓐ bored

  ⓑ amazed

  ⓒ sorry

  ⓓ worried

D What will Juana probably do next?

  ⓐ ask the guard for help

  ⓑ explore the museum alone

  ⓒ stay in the dinosaur room

  ⓓ pretend she is not lost

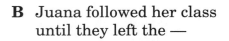
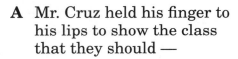

This kind of story usually has two kinds of questions. One kind of question is about the **characters** — the people, or sometimes animals — in the story. Questions about the characters may ask how a character feels about something, what kind of person the character is, or why a character does something in the story.

Example A asks why Mr. Cruz held his finger to his lips. The passage says that he held his finger to his lips "until his students were quiet." So he probably did it to get his students to quiet down, choice Ⓐ. After they were quiet, he asked them to stay together, choice Ⓑ.

Example B asks when Juana stopped following her class. The story says that she kept up with the class until they entered the dinosaur room. She stared at the skeleton for a long time, and then she asked a question. But no one answered because the class was gone. So the answer to this question is choice Ⓒ.

She followed her class until they left the dinosaur room.

Example C asks how Juana felt when she saw the dinosaur skeleton. The passage says that the skeleton was "taller than her house," and Juana had "never seen anything like this before." So Juana probably felt amazed by such a sight. Choice Ⓑ is correct. There is nothing in the story to suggest that she was bored, sorry, or worried by the sight of the dinosaur.

The other kind of question is about the **plot**, or the events that happen in the story. Questions about the plot ask about what happens in the story, or what might happen next.

Example D asks you to guess what will happen next. At the end of the story, Juana realized she was lost and wondered what to do. Then she noticed a museum guard by the doorway, and the guard looked friendly. So she probably will ask the guard for help. Choice Ⓐ is correct.

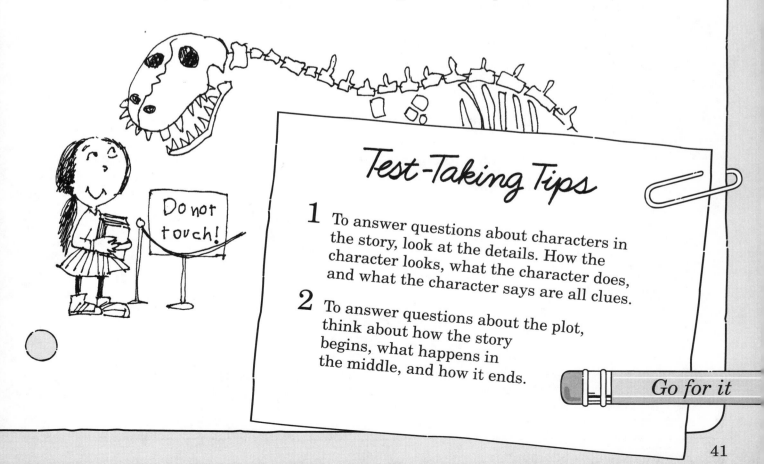

Do not touch!

Test-Taking Tips

1 To answer questions about characters in the story, look at the details. How the character looks, what the character does, and what the character says are all clues.

2 To answer questions about the plot, think about how the story begins, what happens in the middle, and how it ends.

Go for it

Test Practice 11: Characters and Plot

Time: **8** minutes

Directions: Read the passage. Then choose the best answer to each question.

Jim and Aunt Pat did not talk much as they drove down Beacon Street toward the city park. Jim was too busy thinking about pitching in the last baseball game of the summer. If his team won the game, they would be the city champions. Aunt Pat was Jim's biggest fan, and she knew how nervous he was about the game. She had promised to get Jim to the park for an early practice. Lou, the team catcher, was going to meet Jim there so they could warm up together.

Suddenly Jim heard a loud pop and the car swerved. Aunt Pat pulled the car over to the side of the road. "We've got a flat tire," she said. "It's going to take me a while to change it."

Jim stood next to the car as Aunt Pat pulled a spare tire and some tools out of the trunk. He waited silently as his aunt started to remove the flat tire. Then he looked at his watch and sighed. Aunt Pat looked up at him. "Try not to get upset, Jim," she said. "I'll be finished soon. Everything will be fine."

As she spoke, another car pulled up behind them. Lou and his father got out of the car. Jim's face brightened when he saw them. "Boy, am I ever glad to see you!" he cried.

"Lou to the rescue," Aunt Pat said, smiling as she stood up. "You three go on ahead to the park. You don't want to be late. I'll get there before the game starts."

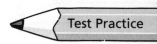

1. At the beginning of this story, what is Jim doing?

   Ⓐ talking to Lou
   Ⓑ riding to the baseball game
   Ⓒ practicing with Lou
   Ⓓ playing catch with his aunt

2. Jim and Lou wanted to get to the park early so they could —

   Ⓐ see some of the other teams play
   Ⓑ warm up before the game
   Ⓒ talk to other players on the team
   Ⓓ take a walk in the park

3. Jim is the kind of boy who —

   Ⓐ wants to do his best
   Ⓑ doesn't get nervous
   Ⓒ tries to cause trouble
   Ⓓ is lazy and careless

4. As Jim and Aunt Pat drove to the park, they —

   Ⓐ ran out of gas
   Ⓑ hit another car
   Ⓒ got a flat tire
   Ⓓ took a wrong turn

5. Aunt Pat pulled over to the side of the road to —

   Ⓐ wait for Lou and his father
   Ⓑ talk to Jim about the game
   Ⓒ change the flat tire
   Ⓓ leave Jim at the park

6. How did Jim feel when he looked at his watch?

   Ⓐ frightened
   Ⓑ silly
   Ⓒ confused
   Ⓓ worried

7. Aunt Pat is the kind of person who —

   Ⓐ gets angry easily
   Ⓑ can't solve problems
   Ⓒ stays calm and relaxed
   Ⓓ is shy and quiet

8. How did Jim feel when he saw Lou and his father?

   Ⓐ relieved
   Ⓑ upset
   Ⓒ tired
   Ⓓ proud

9. What will Jim probably do next?

   Ⓐ Help Aunt Pat fix the tire.
   Ⓑ Ride to the park with Lou.
   Ⓒ Ask Lou and his father to wait with him.
   Ⓓ Walk home with Aunt Pat.

10. What will Aunt Pat do next?

   Ⓐ walk to the park
   Ⓑ leave her car by the road
   Ⓒ take a bus home
   Ⓓ finish changing the tire

Number Correct/Total = _____ /10

Reading Literature

Recognizing types of literature and their characteristics

Directions: Read the passage. Then choose the best answer to each question.

Mary sat beside Pa as he drove the covered wagon along the dusty trail. The horses were getting tired, and they would have to stop soon to rest. In the back of the wagon Mama held baby Emma in her arms.

Although the Crocker family had left St. Louis only ten days before, it seemed like forever to Mary. The long, bumpy ride made her legs feel as stiff as sticks. Her empty stomach growled, too. Last night the family had eaten their last bits of food. Now they were just a few miles from Fort Maynard, where they would get food for the rest of their journey to Oregon. Pa winked at Mary as they rode along. "There's no turning back now," he said.

Mary tried to smile back at Pa. She thought of their neighbors from back home. They had left for Oregon three months ago, and they would soon be her neighbors again in a new home. Mary wondered what this new place would be like. She hoped it would be worth all the trouble they had gone through to get there.

A What is the main problem in this story?

 Ⓐ The horses are tired.

 Ⓑ Mary and her Pa do not get along very well.

 Ⓒ Mary is tired of traveling.

 Ⓓ Their neighbors left three months ago.

B Mary's legs felt "as stiff as sticks" means that Mary was —

 Ⓐ sore and uncomfortable

 Ⓑ holding some sticks

 Ⓒ very tall and thin

 Ⓓ standing up straight

C What kind of story is this?

 Ⓐ historical fiction

 Ⓑ science fiction

 Ⓒ a fairy tale

 Ⓓ a mystery

D What is the message of this story?

 Ⓐ Oregon is a wonderful place.

 Ⓑ Traveling can be exciting.

 Ⓒ It's nice to have neighbors when you need help.

 Ⓓ Moving to a new home is hard.

These kinds of questions are about **reading literature**: the setting and structure of a story, language used by the author, different kinds of literature, and the theme of the story.

Some questions ask about the setting and structure of the story. The **setting** is where and when the story takes place. From the details you can tell that this story takes place on a wagon trail many years ago.

The **structure** of the story is its organization, or how it is put together. In many stories, there is a problem and then a solution. Example A asks what the main problem is in this story. Most of the story is about the difficulties of the trip and how Mary feels about traveling. So answer Ⓒ is correct, *Mary is tired of traveling*. Choices Ⓐ and Ⓓ are details from the story. The structure of the story does not suggest that choice Ⓑ is true.

When writing stories, authors use different kinds of **language** to make the story more interesting. Some questions ask what the author's language means. In Example B, you must decide what the author means by saying that Mary's legs felt "as stiff as sticks." The story says the ride was long and bumpy, so Mary was probably *sore and uncomfortable*, choice Ⓐ.

Some questions, as in Example C, ask about what **kind of literature** you have read. You know that Mary and her family are traveling in a wagon drawn by horses. They won't be able to find any food until they get to a fort up ahead. And they left St. Louis ten days ago. From these clues, you can figure out that the story took place long ago, so it is *historical fiction*, choice Ⓐ.

In some stories, the author is trying to give us a message, or teach us a lesson — often called the **theme**. To answer Example D, you must decide what the author is trying to say in this story. The story tells about the hard journey and how Mary feels about the unknown place that will be her new home. These details suggest that the theme of this story is *Moving to a new home is hard*, so answer Ⓓ is correct.

Test-Taking Tips

1 Figure out what kind of story you are reading by looking for details. Could this story really happen? When does the story take place? Could the characters be real people?

2 The words and phrases that a writer uses in a piece of literature are very important, especially in poetry. Sometimes you will have to figure out what a writer means when you come across words or phrases that create images, such as "legs stiff as sticks." Watch for expressions that don't mean exactly what the words say.

Go for it

Test Practice 12: Reading Literature

Time: **8** minutes

Directions: Read the passage. Then choose the best answer to each question.

Tony sat at a table in his grandfather's restaurant with a drawing pad on his lap. From time to time he looked up at a man who was eating his breakfast at the next table. The man's hair was snowy white, and his face was a spider's web of lines. Tony's pencil moved quickly across his pad as he drew the man's face.

Just then Tony heard his father calling him. He put down his pad and hurried into the kitchen. "Grandpa and I need some help in here," his father said. "Bring up some bread from downstairs. Then start washing these breakfast dishes so we'll be ready for lunch." As Tony started down the stairs, he heard his father say, "Dad, I just don't know what to do about that boy. He'll never learn how to work in this restaurant. He's too busy dreaming about being an artist."

A few minutes later, Tony came back upstairs with the bread. With his father's words ringing in his ears, he started washing the dishes. Then he felt Grandpa's hand on his shoulder. In a kind, gentle voice, Grandpa said, "Never mind what your father says. Sure, it's important to help out around here and learn how to work. But anyone can work in a restaurant. You have a special talent. You're going to be a fine artist. Someday your father will see that. So no matter what happens, don't give up your dream."

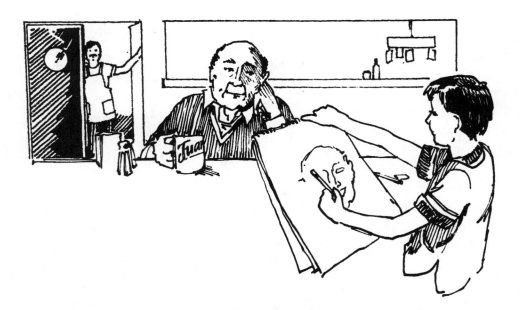

1. When does this story take place?

   Ⓐ after dinner

   Ⓑ in late afternoon

   Ⓒ during lunch

   Ⓓ in the morning

2. What is the main problem in this story?

   Ⓐ Grandpa thinks that Tony has a special talent.

   Ⓑ Tony wants to get a job.

   Ⓒ Tony's father doesn't understand Tony's dream.

   Ⓓ Tony is not a good artist.

3. The man's face "was a spider web of lines" means that —

   Ⓐ the man looked angry

   Ⓑ Tony was drawing a spider

   Ⓒ the man had many wrinkles

   Ⓓ there was a spider on the man's face

4. As Tony washed the dishes, his father's words were "ringing in his ears." This phrase means that Tony —

   Ⓐ heard the telephone ring

   Ⓑ was remembering what his father said

   Ⓒ sang a song to himself

   Ⓓ was listening to the radio

5. When Grandpa speaks in "a kind, gentle voice," you know that he —

   Ⓐ thinks Tony is being silly

   Ⓑ wants to make Tony feel better

   Ⓒ wishes that Tony would work harder

   Ⓓ doesn't want Tony's father to hear what he says

6. This story shows that —

   Ⓐ fathers and sons don't always agree

   Ⓑ families should stay together

   Ⓒ fathers and sons are exactly alike

   Ⓓ some things never change

7. What is the lesson of this story?

   Ⓐ Grown-ups are wiser than young people.

   Ⓑ People should do what is most important to them.

   Ⓒ Hard work can be fun.

   Ⓓ Many people are good artists.

8. What kind of story is this?

   Ⓐ a fairy tale

   Ⓑ science fiction

   Ⓒ a fable

   Ⓓ a real-life story

Number Correct/Total = _____ /8

*This test will tell you how well you might score on a standardized reading test **after** using this book. If you compare your scores on Tryout Tests 1 and 2, you'll see how much you've learned!*

Reading Tryout Test 2

Time: **20** minutes

Directions: Follow the directions for each part of the test. Read each question carefully and fill in the circle beside the answer you choose. The answer to the sample question (**S**) has been filled in for you.

Questions 1–14. Look at the key word. One or more letters are underlined. Find the word that has the same sound as the underlined letters.

S pa<u>th</u>

  Ⓐ trap
  Ⓑ other
  ● thin

1. lau<u>gh</u>ing

  Ⓐ through
  Ⓑ stiff
  Ⓒ bright

2. tha<u>nk</u>

  Ⓐ knit
  Ⓑ monkey
  Ⓒ neck

3. lo<u>s</u>e

  Ⓐ face
  Ⓑ kiss
  Ⓒ size

4. s<u>ch</u>ool

  Ⓐ desk
  Ⓑ cheer
  Ⓒ wish

5. <u>c</u>lean

  Ⓐ walked
  Ⓑ lucky
  Ⓒ exclaim

6. n<u>ew</u>est

  Ⓐ wall
  Ⓑ draw
  Ⓒ wrong

7. <u>c</u>arrot

  Ⓐ track
  Ⓑ wrong
  Ⓒ coat

8. sta<u>y</u>

  Ⓐ fast
  Ⓑ card
  Ⓒ date

9. st<u>oo</u>d

  Ⓐ cook
  Ⓑ tool
  Ⓒ house

10. <u>a</u>part

  Ⓐ faster
  Ⓑ canoe
  Ⓒ raining

11. r<u>ea</u>dy

  Ⓐ heat
  Ⓑ less
  Ⓒ dear

12. t<u>i</u>me

  Ⓐ flying
  Ⓑ spill
  Ⓒ third

13. ret<u>ur</u>n

  Ⓐ build
  Ⓑ must
  Ⓒ chirp

14. l<u>ou</u>d

  Ⓐ tower
  Ⓑ doll
  Ⓒ older

GO ON

Questions 15–18. Find the word or group of words that means the same as the underlined word.

15. Ache means the same as —

ⓐ hurt ⓒ help

ⓑ rub ⓓ find

16. To crumble is to —

ⓐ make noise ⓒ stir up

ⓑ fall apart ⓓ let go

17. A breeze is a —

ⓐ short time ⓒ deep sigh

ⓑ loud sound ⓓ soft wind

18. Sorrow means the same as —

ⓐ anger ⓒ sadness

ⓑ kindness ⓓ respect

Questions 19–20. Find the word that means the OPPOSITE of the underlined word.

19. insult someone

ⓐ trust ⓒ praise

ⓑ like ⓓ teach

20. my enemy

ⓐ friend ⓒ opponent

ⓑ family ⓓ boss

Questions 21–22. Find the word that means the same as the underlined word in the sentence.

21. A dark cloud concealed the sun. Concealed means —

ⓐ warmed ⓒ followed

ⓑ hid ⓓ brightened

22. I felt drowsy, so I took a nap. Drowsy means —

ⓐ nervous ⓒ sleepy

ⓑ sick ⓓ hungry

Questions 23–24. Read the sentence in the box. Then find the sentence in which the underlined word has the same meaning.

23. Place the book on the table.

ⓐ I hope I win first place.

ⓑ Set a place for Aunt Peg.

ⓒ Find a place to sit down.

ⓓ May I place my bag here?

24. The umpire made the call, and the batter was out.

ⓐ It is your call to decide if we should stay or go.

ⓑ Call me when you get home.

ⓒ The little boy tried to call out, but he was frightened.

ⓓ I have to make a telephone call.

49

Reading Tryout Test 2 (continued)

Questions 25–36. Read each passage. Choose the best answer to each question.

For hundreds of years, people have dreamed of building robots that can do the jobs that people do. Now the dream is beginning to come true. In many factories, robots do the kind of work that is too dangerous for people. Other robots do jobs that people find boring. Robots have even been sent to Mars to take pictures and collect soil samples.

However, there are not many robots yet because they are very expensive to build. To work by itself, a robot must have a built-in computer to tell it what to do. A computer that is small enough to fit inside a robot costs a lot of money.

There is also another problem with building robots. Unlike robots you may have seen in movies, real robots can only do simple jobs, such as pulling and lifting. It will be many years before scientists build a robot that can do many different chores. Until then, you will have to make your bed and clean your room by yourself.

25. What is the best title for this passage?

   Ⓐ "Dreaming About Robots"
   Ⓑ "Robots on Mars"
   Ⓒ "A Robot for Your House"
   Ⓓ "Robots of Today"

26. How are all robots alike?

   Ⓐ They take pictures.
   Ⓑ They have built-in computers.
   Ⓒ They do many chores.
   Ⓓ They are used in factories.

27. The author probably thinks that robots —

   Ⓐ are silly machines
   Ⓑ will be used more in the future
   Ⓒ are smarter than workers
   Ⓓ will cause problems for people

28. You would probably read this passage in a book about —

   Ⓐ make-believe people
   Ⓑ history
   Ⓒ people of other lands
   Ⓓ science

GO ON

On sunny days, my shadow comes
And copies every move I make.
A flat gray shape upon the ground,
It never talks or makes a sound.

On cloudy days, my shadow fades,
I wonder where it likes to go.
Perhaps it plays with shadow friends
Till sunshine calls it back again.

29. This poem is mostly about —

Ⓐ the sun

Ⓑ a shadow

Ⓒ gray clouds

Ⓓ a friend

30. The speaker in this poem feels —

Ⓐ tired of having a shadow

Ⓑ curious about what happens to the shadow

Ⓒ frightened of the shadow

Ⓓ worried that the shadow will go away

31. The shadow comes when —

Ⓐ the speaker moves

Ⓑ it hears a sound

Ⓒ the sun is shining

Ⓓ it touches the ground

32. Which sentence tells about something that could NOT really happen?

Ⓐ On sunny days I see my shadow.

Ⓑ It looks flat and gray.

Ⓒ The shadow fades away.

Ⓓ The shadow plays with its friends.

51

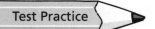

Reading Tryout Test 2 (continued)

Danny and Jay had been best friends ever since the first grade. They never had to do anything special to have fun. They just enjoyed playing together. Then a new boy, Nate Gleason, moved in next door to Danny. Soon Danny and Nate began spending a lot of time together. Almost every weekend, Nate's father took the boys to a movie, a ball game, a museum, or an amusement park. At first Danny felt bad about leaving Jay out of the fun. By the time summer came, though, Danny had almost forgotten about his old friend.

One day Nate stopped by Danny's house. "I just came to say good-bye," Nate said. "I'm going to visit my cousins for a month. I'll see you in August."

From the window, Danny watched Nate's car until it was out of sight. "What am I going to do with myself for a month?" he wondered. Then he thought about his old friend. He had not seen Jay for quite a while, but he picked up the phone and dialed Jay's number. When Jay answered the phone, Danny said, "Hi, Jay, this is Danny. Would you like to do something with me today?"

At first Jay was silent. Then he said, "It's great to hear from you, Danny."

33. What will probably happen next?

  Ⓐ Danny and Jay will play together.

  Ⓑ Jay will go away to visit his cousins.

  Ⓒ Danny will call Nate.

  Ⓓ Jay will make friends with Nate.

34. What is the theme of this story?

  Ⓐ No one should have two different friends.

  Ⓑ Making new friends is easy.

  Ⓒ People should not forget their old friends.

  Ⓓ Young boys love to go to amusement parks.

35. From reading this story, you know that —

  Ⓐ Nate did not like Jay

  Ⓑ Danny enjoyed the things he did with Nate

  Ⓒ Jay made other friends

  Ⓓ Nate and Danny will always be best friends

36. Why did Danny call Jay?

  Ⓐ He wanted to do something special and fun.

  Ⓑ He felt sorry for Jay.

  Ⓒ He wanted to tell Jay about Nate.

  Ⓓ He was lonely and bored.

Number Correct/Total = _____ /36

Language Arts

53

Top Ten Language Arts Tips

1 Read all DIRECTIONS through twice. Directions for language arts items often tell you to look for answer choices that have *mistakes* or *errors*. Other times, you are asked to look for the answer with *no mistakes*. It is important to know exactly what to look for.

2 Watch out for negative words in the directions, such as NOT or OPPOSITE. These words tell you exactly what answer to look for. Such words often appear in **bold** or *italic* type, or in ALL CAPITAL LETTERS.

3 When asked to answer questions about a reading passage, read the *questions* first. That way, you'll know what to look for as you read the passage. When you finish the passage, go on to answer the questions.

4 In language arts questions, look for key words, such as *who, what, when, where, why,* and *how,* that will help you answer each question. This is especially important when answering questions about maps, charts, and graphs or reference sources, such as dictionary entries, indexes, and tables of contents.

5 When answering questions about maps, charts, graphs, or reference sources, such as dictionary entries, always look back at the diagram or sample reference to answer the questions. Don't just rely on your memory.

6 Questions dealing with capitalization and punctuation can be tricky. The answer choices often look very much alike. Read *all* the answer choices, and choose your answer carefully.

7 For fill-in sentences, try each answer choice in the blank to see which one sounds right or makes the most sense.

8 For fill-in sentences, always read the entire sentence before you choose an answer. Use context clues, other words in the sentence that help define the unknown word, to find the correct answer.

9 When looking for word meanings, or definitions, use context clues to help you decide which definition of a word is best.

10 When asked to identify order of events, look for key words that signal time sequence, for example: *first, next, then, after, finally,* and *at last.*

Language Arts Tryout Test 1

Time: 30 minutes

Directions: Follow the directions for each part of the test. Read each question carefully and fill in the circle for the answer you choose. The answer to the sample question (**S**) has been filled in for you.

Questions 1–5. Choose the word or group of words that best completes the sentence.

S Next week Sasha _____ her hair cut for the first time.

Ⓐ got
Ⓑ getting
● will get
Ⓓ had gotten

1. Mark _____ followed the footprints through the woods.

Ⓐ carefully
Ⓑ most careful
Ⓒ careful
Ⓓ carefuller

2. Please give the keys to _____.

Ⓐ she and I
Ⓑ her and me
Ⓒ me and her
Ⓓ I and she

3. Five cherry trees _____ in the park.

Ⓐ grows
Ⓑ has grown
Ⓒ does grow
Ⓓ grow

4. Which of the two girls is _____?

Ⓐ most tall
Ⓑ tallest
Ⓒ more tall
Ⓓ taller

5. Is this blue mitten Kelly's or _____?

Ⓐ yours
Ⓑ your
Ⓒ you
Ⓓ yourself

Questions 6–7. Choose the simple subject of the sentence.

6. In the <u>evening</u>, <u>bats</u> <u>fly</u> around our <u>house</u>.
    Ⓐ   Ⓑ   Ⓒ   Ⓓ

7. <u>Jessica</u> <u>gave</u> <u>catnip</u> and a toy mouse to her <u>kitten</u>.
    Ⓐ   Ⓑ   Ⓒ   Ⓓ

GO ON

Language Arts Tryout Test 1 (continued)

Questions 8–9. Choose the simple predicate of the sentence.

---

8. All the <u>students</u> and their <u>parents</u> <u>met</u> the new <u>teacher</u>.
   Ⓐ   Ⓑ Ⓒ   Ⓓ

9. The <u>runner</u> <u>fell</u> on the <u>ground</u> <u>after</u> the race.
  Ⓐ Ⓑ   Ⓒ Ⓓ

Questions 10–11. Read the four groups of words. Choose the one that is a complete sentence written correctly.

---

10. Ⓐ The babysitter knocked at the front door she came in.
  Ⓑ Played cards with Jeremy and Jonathan.
  Ⓒ She took them upstairs she told them a ghost story.
  Ⓓ Jonathan was too scared to fall asleep!

11. Ⓐ A chameleon a type of lizard.
  Ⓑ A chameleon can change its color.
  Ⓒ They are usually green they can turn dark gray.
  Ⓓ Many skin colors including orange and yellow.

Questions 12–13. Read the underlined sentences. Choose the answer that best combines them into one clear sentence without changing their meaning.

---

12. <u>Uncle Will carried a suitcase.</u>
 <u>The suitcase was ancient.</u>

  Ⓐ Uncle Will carried a suitcase and it was ancient.
  Ⓑ Ancient Uncle Will carried a suitcase.
  Ⓒ Uncle Will carried an ancient suitcase.
  Ⓓ The ancient suitcase and Uncle Will carried it.

13. <u>Panthers run fast.</u>
 <u>Jaguars run fast.</u>

  Ⓐ Panthers and jaguars run fast.
  Ⓑ Panthers run fast and jaguars.
  Ⓒ Run fast panthers and jaguars.
  Ⓓ Panthers run fast and also jaguars.

GO ON

Questions 14–15. Read the paragraph and answer the question.

14.   Wild turkeys are very difficult to catch. They have excellent sight and hearing. _____ If they see an enemy, they run or fly away at high speed.

Which sentence fits best in the paragraph?

  Ⓐ Tame turkeys are slow, plump, stupid birds.

  Ⓑ They have dark feathers and bald, red heads.

  Ⓒ They are afraid of people and other animals.

  Ⓓ Early explorers in America sent turkeys back to Europe.

15. [1]Aunt Mabel sewed the hemmed squares into a quilt.

  [2]She hemmed the edges of each square.

  [3]Aunt Mabel got out a bunch of old shirts and dresses.

  [4]She cut the clothing up into four-inch squares.

In which order would the sentences make the best paragraph?

  Ⓐ 3 - 4 - 2 - 1   Ⓒ 1 - 2 - 3 - 4

  Ⓑ 4 - 2 - 1 - 3   Ⓓ 3 - 1 - 2 - 4

Questions 16–19. Read the phrases. In one of the phrases, the underlined word is misspelled for the way it is used. Choose the phrase in which the underlined word is NOT spelled correctly.

16. Ⓐ nail the <u>bored</u>

    Ⓑ stub your <u>toe</u>

    Ⓒ the middle of the <u>night</u>

    Ⓓ the oldest <u>son</u>

17. Ⓐ cloudy <u>days</u>

    Ⓑ <u>not</u> enough food

    Ⓒ <u>whose</u> socks

    Ⓓ a pile of <u>would</u>

18. Ⓐ <u>dew</u> on the leaves

    Ⓑ never <u>seen</u> lightning

    Ⓒ the <u>reign</u> falling

    Ⓓ <u>through</u> the fog

19. Ⓐ a <u>lone</u> of ten dollars

    Ⓑ <u>to</u> the fair

    Ⓒ <u>their</u> sisters

    Ⓓ <u>your</u> friend

GO ON

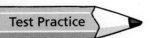

Language Arts Tryout Test 1 (continued)

Questions 20–25. Read each sentence. Choose the sentence that uses correct punctuation and capitalization.

20. Ⓐ I go to the Jamestown Elementary school.
    Ⓑ each June, a famous person comes to the school.
    Ⓒ A great basketball player visited on June 12, 1990.
    Ⓓ His name is C F Morrison and he plays for the Eagles.

21. Ⓐ A new boy named Gus meyer moved in next door.
    Ⓑ I invited him to meet me at Green Park on Saturday.
    Ⓒ He said "I don't know where that is."
    Ⓓ I told him it was across from noah's restaurant.

22. Ⓐ Lately Tom Zizka hasnt been able to sleep at night.
    Ⓑ Tom got a scottish terrier for his birthday.
    Ⓒ The dog barks growls and whines all night.
    Ⓓ Tom's mother says the dog is worse than a baby.

23. Ⓐ The postcard from Nana was dated Oct 16, 1991.
    Ⓑ Nomi tried to read the message but couldn't.
    Ⓒ Nanas handwriting looked like spider tracks.
    Ⓓ Was Nana visiting austria or australia?

24. Ⓐ Tyler, Kate, and Megan want to see *The Sandman*.
    Ⓑ The movie is playing at the niantic theater.
    Ⓒ Tyler's mom said, I can take you kids tomorrow.
    Ⓓ In the dark theater, they waited for the movie?

25. Ⓐ Everybody loves doctor Kundrat.
    Ⓑ He treats kids like theyre old friends.
    Ⓒ When I walk in he always says, "How are you, Annie?"
    Ⓓ I think he is the best doctor in Chicago Illinois.

Questions 26–29. Read and answer each question.

26. Which word comes first in alphabetical order?

    Ⓐ tin
    Ⓑ timid
    Ⓒ ticket
    Ⓓ title

27. Which word is a main heading that includes the other words?

    Ⓐ sport
    Ⓑ tennis
    Ⓒ baseball
    Ⓓ soccer

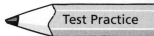

28. If you want to find the meaning of the word *flimsy*, you should look in —

   Ⓐ an atlas

   Ⓑ a dictionary

   Ⓒ an encyclopedia

   Ⓓ a telephone book

29. If you want to find information about the life of Martin Luther King, you should look in —

   Ⓐ a dictionary

   Ⓑ an atlas

   Ⓒ a telephone book

   Ⓓ an encyclopedia

Questions 30–31. Use the table of contents to answer each question.

CONTENTS

30. Which chapter has information about hurricanes?

   Ⓐ 1   Ⓒ 3

   Ⓑ 2   Ⓓ 4

31. On what page does Chapter 4 begin?

   Ⓐ 14   Ⓒ 48

   Ⓑ 31   Ⓓ 62

Questions 32–35. Use the sample dictionary entries to answer each question.

cream [krēm] *n.* 1. the part of milk that contains fat and is yellowish. 2. a substance used to soften skin. 3. the best of something. 4. a yellowish white color.

cre·ate [krē āt′] *v.* To make, or cause to happen.

cre·a·tion [krē ā′ shən] *n.* 1. the act of creating. 2. something that has been created.

cress [krĕs] *n.* a plant sometimes used in salad.

32. *Cress* is a kind of —

   Ⓐ drink   Ⓒ plant

   Ⓑ color   Ⓓ milk

33. To *create* means to —

   Ⓐ make   Ⓒ separate

   Ⓑ soften   Ⓓ contain

34. Which definition of *cream* best fits the sentence below?

   The bedroom walls are *cream*.

   Ⓐ 1   Ⓒ 3

   Ⓑ 2   Ⓓ 4

35. Which word is spelled correctly?

   Ⓐ creem   Ⓒ cres

   Ⓑ create   Ⓓ creashun

Number Correct/Total = _____ /35

Parts of Speech

Identifying and using correct word forms in sentences

Directions: Choose the word or words that best complete the sentence.

A Dottie is the _____ of our three cats.

    Ⓐ smart

    Ⓑ smarterest

    Ⓒ smarter

    Ⓓ smartest

B She _____ how to open the door.

    Ⓐ knows

    Ⓑ knowing

    Ⓒ know

    Ⓓ knowed

Example A tests the use of **adjectives**, or describing words. Since three cats are being described in the sentence, you should pick an adjective that ends with *est*. The correct answer is choice Ⓓ, *smartest*. (Choice Ⓑ, *smarterest*, is not a real word.)

Example B is a question about **verbs**, or action words. The verb in a sentence must always match the subject. In this question, the correct answer is Ⓐ, she *knows*.

Now look at this example.

Directions: Read the sentences. Choose the sentence that is written correctly.

C Ⓐ Dad built a ladder for her and I.

    Ⓑ Them don't have a ladder.

    Ⓒ Invite him and her to play.

    Ⓓ They invited we to swim.

For Example C, choice Ⓒ is the correct answer. It is the only sentence that is written correctly.

Language Rules

▶ Use the correct form of the verb to show when something happens.

José **played** soccer yesterday.

Today José **plays** baseball.

Tomorrow he **will play** football.

▶ The verb must always agree with the subject.

She lives on Maple Road.

They live on Elm Street.

▶ With adjectives, use the *er* ending or the word *more* when comparing two things. Use the *est* ending or *most* when comparing more than two things.

Jupiter is **larger** than Mars. It is also **more interesting**.

Jupiter is the **largest** and **most interesting** of the nine planets.

▶ Use a subject pronoun to show who or what does something: *I, we, you, he, she, they*. If you use two or more pronouns including *I*, write *I* last.

He and **I** went on the roller coaster.

▶ Use an object pronoun to show to whom or to what it is done: *me, us, you, them, him,* and *her*. If you use two or more pronouns including *me*, write *me* last.

Mom bought Popsicles for **him** and **me**.

Test-Taking Tips

1 For verb forms, try out each answer in the sentence. Choose the one that sounds right. An answer that sounds strange is probably wrong.

2 Watch out for irregular forms of words (such as *knew*), and answer choices which are not real words (such as *smarterest* and *knowed*).

3 Watch out for the most common kinds of mistakes (for example, "They invited *we* to swim" instead of "They invited *us*").

Go for it

Test Practice 1: Parts of Speech

Time: **15** minutes

Questions 1–10. Read each sentence. Choose the word
or words that best complete the sentence.

1. Rick _____ a bullfrog at the edge of the pond.

   Ⓐ caught
   Ⓑ catched
   Ⓒ catch
   Ⓓ catching

2. The robin _____ a nest in the maple tree.

   Ⓐ have built
   Ⓑ build
   Ⓒ are building
   Ⓓ builds

3. Next week workers _____ for a well in our yard.

   Ⓐ drilled
   Ⓑ drilling
   Ⓒ will drill
   Ⓓ have drilled

4. A kite sailed _____ through the air.

   Ⓐ light
   Ⓑ lightly
   Ⓒ lighter
   Ⓓ lightest

5. Of the three villains, the Weasel seemed _____.

   Ⓐ most terrible
   Ⓑ terribly
   Ⓒ more terrible
   Ⓓ terriblest

6. Marie put _____ in the soup.

   Ⓐ an onion and a carrot
   Ⓑ a onion and a carrot
   Ⓒ an onion and an carrot
   Ⓓ a onion and an carrot

7. The pilot showed _____ how to steer the airplane.

   Ⓐ they
   Ⓑ her and he
   Ⓒ them
   Ⓓ she and him

8. _____ teddy bear has a missing eye.

   Ⓐ Mine
   Ⓑ Myself
   Ⓒ Me
   Ⓓ My

9. _____ jumped each time lightning lit the sky.

   Ⓐ She and me
   Ⓑ She and I
   Ⓒ Me and her
   Ⓓ I and she

10. I tried to wind the clock, _____ the key broke off.

    Ⓐ nor
    Ⓑ or
    Ⓒ but
    Ⓓ either

GO ON

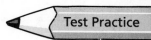

Questions 11–18. Read each group of sentences.
Choose the sentence that is written correctly.

11. Ⓐ Two woman entered the elevator.
    Ⓑ A boy was standing in the front.
    Ⓒ He politely pushed one buttons.
    Ⓓ Both door slid silently shut.

12. Ⓐ Until last week, I never seen an alligator.
    Ⓑ Last Tuesday, I will be visiting Granddad in North Carolina.
    Ⓒ Granddad and I fishing in a big lake.
    Ⓓ Suddenly an alligator poked its nose up at us!

13. Ⓐ Leonard and Bobby is twins.
    Ⓑ Even the mother of the twins get them mixed up.
    Ⓒ There is just one way to tell them apart.
    Ⓓ Bobby have a small scar on his chin.

14. Ⓐ The brightly stars shone.
    Ⓑ A gentle breeze blew.
    Ⓒ The flowers smelled sweetly.
    Ⓓ An owl hooted mysterious.

15. Ⓐ Of the three pups, Flan was the most lovable.
    Ⓑ Mick's fur was curliest than Clover's.
    Ⓒ Clover had the louder bark of the three.
    Ⓓ Flan had the mostest fleas of the pups!

16. Ⓐ Place your order with an waiter.
    Ⓑ First ask for a glass of milk.
    Ⓒ They serve a excellent beef stew here.
    Ⓓ Would you like a ice cream cone for dessert?

17. Ⓐ Mom took Elena and I to the circus.
    Ⓑ Were you and her there, too?
    Ⓒ Me and Elena liked the clowns the best.
    Ⓓ She whispered to me, "Look at the clown with the big shoes!"

18. Ⓐ The guide showed Jason and me a robin's nest.
    Ⓑ I and Jason asked how the bird made the nest.
    Ⓒ The guide showed me and Jason bits of string and straw.
    Ⓓ Me and Jason asked if the bird made the nest with its beak.

Number Correct/Total = _____ /18

63

Sentence Parts

Recognizing subjects, predicates, and correct word order

Directions: Choose the simple subject of the sentence.

A The hurricane blew the roof off the school.
   Ⓐ Ⓑ   Ⓒ   Ⓓ

Example A asks you to find the simple subject of the sentence. The **simple subject** is the person or thing that does something in the sentence. In this sentence, the *hurricane* is the thing that "blew." So choice Ⓐ, *hurricane*, is the correct answer.

Now look at this example.

Directions: Choose the simple predicate of the sentence.

B Mr. Celebrese fixed the roof last week.
    Ⓐ Ⓑ   Ⓒ Ⓓ

Example B asks you to find the simple predicate. The **simple predicate** is the verb that tells what the person or thing does in the sentence. In this example, Mr. Celebrese *fixed* the roof. *Fixed* tells what he did. So choice Ⓑ, *fixed*, is correct.

Directions: Read each sentence. Choose the sentence in which the words are in the correct order.

C Ⓐ The dollhouse is made of cardboard.

  Ⓑ Made of cardboard the dollhouse is.

  Ⓒ Is made of cardboard the dollhouse.

Choice Ⓐ is correct because the words are in correct sentence order.

Test-Taking Tips

1 When looking for the subject, ask yourself *who* (or *what*) is doing something (*the hurricane, Mr. Celebrese*).

2 When looking for the predicate, ask yourself *what* is the person (or thing) doing (*blew, fixed*).

3 In most sentences, the subject comes first and the predicate follows (*The hurricane blew... Mr. Celbrese fixed... The dollhouse is...*).

Go fo

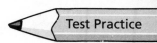

Test Practice 2: Sentence Parts

Time: **20** minutes

Questions 1–6. Choose the simple subject of the sentence.

1. The baby <u>bird</u> <u>fell</u> <u>out</u> of the <u>nest</u>.
         Ⓐ   Ⓑ   Ⓒ   Ⓓ

2. The <u>fiery</u> <u>volcano</u> <u>spit</u> <u>lava</u> into the air.
    Ⓐ   Ⓑ   Ⓒ Ⓓ

3. Behind the <u>curtains</u>, <u>Devon</u> was <u>hiding</u> from his <u>sisters</u>.
           Ⓐ   Ⓑ   Ⓒ   Ⓓ

4. <u>Prairie dogs</u> <u>greet</u> each <u>other</u> with a <u>kiss</u>.
    Ⓐ   Ⓑ   Ⓒ   Ⓓ

5. <u>Luisa</u> took her <u>net</u> to <u>hunt</u> for <u>butterflies</u>.
  Ⓐ   Ⓑ   Ⓒ   Ⓓ

6. After the <u>flood</u>, <u>people</u> <u>shoveled</u> <u>mud</u> from their basements.
        Ⓐ   Ⓑ   Ⓒ   Ⓓ

Questions 7–12. Choose the simple predicate of the sentence.

7. The <u>smiling</u> <u>magician</u> <u>pulled</u> a <u>coin</u> out of Jerry's ear.
      Ⓐ   Ⓑ   Ⓒ   Ⓓ

8. <u>Snow</u> <u>covers</u> the <u>top</u> of the <u>mountain</u>.
  Ⓐ   Ⓑ   Ⓒ   Ⓓ

9. <u>Loud</u> <u>noises</u> <u>bother</u> my <u>mother</u>.
  Ⓐ   Ⓑ   Ⓒ   Ⓓ

10. <u>George</u> <u>wore</u> <u>his</u> Mighty Man <u>t-shirt</u> on the hike.
   Ⓐ   Ⓑ Ⓒ   Ⓓ

11. <u>Oil spills</u> <u>hurt</u> <u>birds</u> <u>and</u> other animals.
    Ⓐ   Ⓑ   Ⓒ Ⓓ

12. The <u>beautiful</u> <u>skater</u> <u>leaped</u> <u>high</u> into the air.
     Ⓐ   Ⓑ   Ⓒ   Ⓓ

GO ON

Questions 13–22. Read each group of sentences. Choose the sentence in which the words are in the correct order.

13. Ⓐ A four-leaf clover found Dirk.
    Ⓑ Dirk a four-leaf clover found.
    Ⓒ Dirk found a four-leaf clover.

14. Ⓐ The motorcycle zoomed down the highway.
    Ⓑ The motorcycle down zoomed the highway.
    Ⓒ The motorcycle the highway zoomed down.

15. Ⓐ Kevin and Ashley out of flour and salt made a map.
    Ⓑ Made a map Kevin and Ashley out of flour and salt.
    Ⓒ Kevin and Ashley made a map out of flour and salt.

16. Ⓐ Danced the poodle on its hind legs.
    Ⓑ The poodle danced on its hind legs.
    Ⓒ The poodle danced its hind legs on.

17. Ⓐ Rhonda on put a pair of green sunglasses.
    Ⓑ A pair of green sunglasses put on Rhonda.
    Ⓒ Rhonda put on a pair of green sunglasses.

18. Ⓐ A comic book gave Mrs. Kravitz each child.
    Ⓑ Mrs. Kravitz gave each child a comic book.
    Ⓒ Mrs. Kravitz each child a comic book gave.

19. Ⓐ Lacy put a bell on her bicycle.
    Ⓑ A bell put Lacy on her bicycle.
    Ⓒ On her bicycle a bell put Lacy.

20. Ⓐ A huge package the mail carrier delivered.
    Ⓑ The mail carrier delivered a huge package.
    Ⓒ The mail carrier a huge package delivered.

21. Ⓐ The bright sun made the bus driver squint.
    Ⓑ The bus driver squint made the bright sun.
    Ⓒ Squint made the bright sun the bus driver.

22. Ⓐ On his toothbrush Sami mint toothpaste put.
    Ⓑ Mint toothpaste put Sami on his toothbrush.
    Ⓒ Sami put mint toothpaste on his toothbrush.

STOP

Number Correct/Total = _____ /22

Sentences

Recognizing complete sentences

eggs

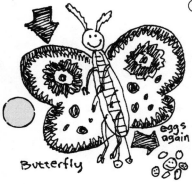
pupa

Directions: Read the four groups of words. Choose the one that is a correct sentence.

A Ⓐ The butterfly's different life stages.

Ⓑ It starts out as an egg it turns into a pupa.

Ⓒ The adult butterfly comes out of the pupa.

Ⓓ Lays more eggs.

B Ⓐ Butterflies are usually brightly colored.

Ⓑ Moths paler colored.

Ⓒ Butterflies fly during the days moths at night.

Ⓓ Feed mostly on liquids.

A **complete sentence** has a subject and a verb, and it expresses a complete thought. In Example A, the correct answer is choice Ⓒ. It has a subject (*The adult butterfly*), a verb (*comes*), and it expresses a complete thought. A sentence that does not have a subject or a verb, or does not express a complete thought, is a **sentence fragment**. Choice Ⓐ is an incomplete sentence because it does not have a verb. Choice Ⓓ is incomplete because it has no subject. Choice Ⓑ is a **run-on sentence** made up of two sentences run together.

In Example B, choice Ⓐ is correct. Choices Ⓑ and Ⓓ are incomplete sentences. Choice Ⓒ is a run-on sentence.

Butterfly

Hints

Look at these examples of a run-on sentence and a sentence fragment. Each one has been rewritten correctly.

Run-on sentence:
The nurse cleaned the cut the doctor stitched it.

Correct:
The nurse cleaned the cut, and the doctor stitched it.

Sentence fragment:
Took out the stitches a week later.

Correct:
The doctor took out the stitches a week later.

Test-Taking Tips

1 Look for the answer choice that has a subject and a verb, and expresses a complete thought. (*The adult butterfly comes out of the pupa.*)

2 Watch out for answer choices in which two sentences are run together without a conjunction (such as *and, but, or*) or proper punctuation. These are run-on sentences.

Go for it

Test Practice 3: Sentences

Time: **15** minutes

Directions: Read the four groups of words.
Choose the one that is a correct sentence.

1. Ⓐ Our neighbors had a small house it had four rooms.
   Ⓑ Decided to build a family room on the back.
   Ⓒ Every member of the family worked on the house.
   Ⓓ The parents hammered and sawed the kids painted.

2. Ⓐ Many important medicines from plants.
   Ⓑ Scientists are still trying to find new plant medicines.
   Ⓒ Rainforests full of unusual plants.
   Ⓓ Rainforests are disappearing this is bad for medicine.

3. Ⓐ Moles are famous for their poor eyesight.
   Ⓑ They don't need to see very well they live underground.
   Ⓒ Good sense of smell and a good sense of touch.
   Ⓓ Powerful front paws for digging tunnels.

4. Ⓐ Today there are seven separate continents.
   Ⓑ Connected together in the distant past.
   Ⓒ They split apart they are still drifting apart from each other.
   Ⓓ Maybe some day southern California a continent.

5. Ⓐ Annette goes to yard sales she collects dolls.
   Ⓑ China dolls, rag dolls, even plastic dolls.
   Ⓒ Knows how to clean and fix dolls so they look new.
   Ⓓ Some of her dolls are very valuable.

6. Ⓐ Different manners in different countries.
   Ⓑ Some people shake hands some people bow.
   Ⓒ Rude to look into a person's eyes while talking.
   Ⓓ Learn the rules of behavior before you travel far away.

7. Ⓐ Amanda and Joel in front of the television.
   Ⓑ They are arguing over what program to watch.
   Ⓒ Mandy wants to watch soccer Joel wants to see "KoolKat."
   Ⓓ Flipping a coin and let the winner choose.

8. Ⓐ The earth has one moon Mars has two.
   Ⓑ One Martian moon is named Phobos the other is Deimos.
   Ⓒ Phobos is shaped like a long potato.
   Ⓓ Both much smaller than our moon.

GO ON

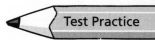

9. Ⓐ Dressing and packing to go to the beach.
   Ⓑ Everybody put on sunscreen they packed swimsuits.
   Ⓒ Towels, magazines, floats, snacks, and umbrellas.
   Ⓓ By the time they got to the beach it was time to leave!

10. Ⓐ This century is famous for many strange works of art.
    Ⓑ Huge dolls covered with live snails and riding in a taxi.
    Ⓒ A bicycle wheel sitting on top of a stool.
    Ⓓ One artist painted squares of color another dribbled paint.

11. Ⓐ When riding a bicycle on a busy street.
    Ⓑ Riders should ride in the direction of the traffic.
    Ⓒ Using hand signals to indicate turns or stops.
    Ⓓ Riders should wear helmets they prevent head injuries.

12. Ⓐ Montana is ten her sister Savannah is eight.
    Ⓑ Both girls love to read they like animal stories.
    Ⓒ Up late one summer night reading *Lassie Come Home*.
    Ⓓ Montana hopes to write her own books one day.

13. Ⓐ A pet hamster in Mr. Lee's third-grade class.
    Ⓑ Named Peaches and Cream because she is orange and white.
    Ⓒ Each weekend one of the students takes her home.
    Ⓓ She likes to run around she nibbles on everything.

14. Ⓐ A playground full of the noises of children playing.
    Ⓑ The sound of jump ropes slapping against the ground.
    Ⓒ One group is playing tag they yell and giggle.
    Ⓓ Somebody whacks a ball across the field.

15. Ⓐ Playful, lovable river otters.
    Ⓑ Few remaining in the rivers of the United States.
    Ⓒ Now scientists are returning otters to many rivers.
    Ⓓ People like to watch them they are friendly animals.

16. Ⓐ Jian climbed the jungle gym she went to the top.
    Ⓑ She hung upside down by her knees.
    Ⓒ Hanging there for at least three minutes.
    Ⓓ A little dizzy when she got down.

Number Correct/Total = _____ /16

Combining Sentences

Revising sentences by combining them

Directions: Read the underlined sentences. Choose the answer that best combines them into one clear sentence without changing their meaning.

Mary Lou has a new bike.
The bike is silver.

    Ⓐ   Mary Lou has a new bike and a silver bike.

    Ⓑ   Also silver was the new bike of Mary Lou.

    Ⓒ   Mary Lou has a new silver bike.

    Ⓓ   The silver bike that Mary Lou has is a new bike, too.

The correct answer is choice Ⓒ. Choice Ⓐ is wrong because it suggests that Mary Lou has two bikes. Choice Ⓑ is wrong because the words are not in the correct order. Choice Ⓓ has the same meaning as the two underlined sentences, but it is long and awkward.

Hints

    These kinds of test questions usually combine sentences by combining subjects, predicates, or modifiers (adjectives or adverbs). Here are some examples.

Carmen likes movies. Nancy likes movies.
Combined subjects:
Carmen and Nancy like movies.

The crow squawked. The crow flew away.
Combined predicates:
The crow squawked and flew away.

The wolf ran swiftly. The wolf ran silently.
Combined modifiers:
The wolf ran swiftly and silently.

Test-Taking Tips

1   Make sure the combined sentence has all of the information that was in the two underlined sentences.

2   Make sure the word order is correct. Words should not be repeated unless they have to be.

3   If a conjunction (such as *and, but, or*) is used, make sure it is the correct one. The wrong conjunction changes the meaning.

Go for i

Test Practice 4: Combining Sentences   Time: 10 minutes

Directions: Read the sentences. Choose the answer that best combines them into one clear sentence without changing their meaning.

1. I collected shells.
   Millie collected shells.

   Ⓐ Collect shells is what Millie and I did.

   Ⓑ Millie and I collected shells.

   Ⓒ Shells, Millie, and I collected.

   Ⓓ I collected shells and Millie.

2. We boiled the eggs.
   We decorated the eggs.

   Ⓐ We boiled the eggs but decorated them.

   Ⓑ We boiled the eggs and we decorated the eggs.

   Ⓒ Boiled and decorated the eggs, we did.

   Ⓓ We boiled and decorated the eggs.

3. Nerissa turned on the radio.
   Al danced.

   Ⓐ Nerissa and Al turned on the radio and danced.

   Ⓑ Nerissa turned on the radio and Al danced.

   Ⓒ Nerissa turned on the radio Al danced.

   Ⓓ Nerissa turned on the radio or Al danced.

4. Sam won a blue ribbon.
   She put it on her wall.

   Ⓐ A blue ribbon was won by Sam, and put on her wall.

   Ⓑ Sam won a blue ribbon, Sam put it on her wall.

   Ⓒ Sam won a blue ribbon and put it on her wall.

   Ⓓ Sam won a blue ribbon and a wall.

5. Cars drove through the fog.
   Cars drove slowly.

   Ⓐ Cars drove slowly through the fog.

   Ⓑ Cars drove through the fog and slowly.

   Ⓒ Through the fog drove slowly the cars.

   Ⓓ The cars that drove slowly drove through the fog.

6. The airplane was large.
   I flew in the airplane.

   Ⓐ The airplane was large and I flew in it.

   Ⓑ The airplane that I flew in and I were large.

   Ⓒ I flew in the large airplane.

   Ⓓ The airplane was large, but I flew in it.

7. Spot did not see the rabbit.
   Spot did not hear the rabbit.

   Ⓐ Spot did not see or hear the rabbit.

   Ⓑ Spot did not see the rabbit that he did not hear.

   Ⓒ The rabbit and Spot did not see or hear.

   Ⓓ Spot did not see the rabbit and Spot did not hear.

8. Juan returned the video.
   Juan paid the fine.

   Ⓐ Juan returned and paid the video fine.

   Ⓑ Juan returned the video and paid the fine.

   Ⓒ Juan returned the paid fine video.

   Ⓓ The video and the fine were returned and paid.

9. The tank is full of fish.
   The fish are bright blue.

   Ⓐ The tank is full of bright blue fish.

   Ⓑ The bright blue tank is full of fish.

   Ⓒ The full tank has fish that are bright blue.

   Ⓓ The fish are in the tank and they are bright blue.

10. Lightning struck close by.
    Our house went dark.

   Ⓐ Lightning struck close by our dark house.

   Ⓑ Our house was dark the lightning struck close by.

   Ⓒ Lightning and our dark house were struck close by.

   Ⓓ Lightning struck close by, and our house went dark.

STOP

Number Correct/Total = _____ /10

Writing Paragraphs

Completing paragraphs and arranging sentences in order

Directions: Read the paragraph and answer the question.

A Many animals sleep during the day and wake at night. Owls are well-known night birds. _____ Moths rest on trees during the day and fly at night.

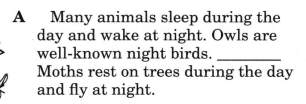

Which sentence best fills the blank in the paragraph?

Ⓐ Some owls are very large, and some are small.

Ⓑ Temperatures are usually cooler at night than during the day.

Ⓒ Raccoons roam around at night, looking for food.

Ⓓ Lizards like to lie in the hot sun during the day.

The first sentence tells what the paragraph is about: animals that sleep during the day and are awake at night. Sentences two and four in the paragraph give examples of animals

like this. So the missing sentence must also give an example. Choice Ⓒ is correct.

Now let's look at a different kind of question. Read the paragraph below.

B ¹She put the dirty sheets in the laundry basket.

²Then Althea carried the basket downstairs.

³First, Althea took the sheets off her bed.

⁴She put the sheets in the washing machine and added soap.

In which order would the sentences make the best paragraph?

Ⓐ 1 – 2 – 3 – 4   Ⓒ 3 – 1 – 2 – 4

Ⓑ 2 – 1 – 3 – 4   Ⓓ 3 – 2 – 1 – 4

The correct answer is choice Ⓒ because it tells the correct order for taking sheets off a bed and washing them.

Test-Taking Tips

1 If you are trying to find the sentence that fits a paragraph, first figure out the main idea of the paragraph. Then find the detail sentence that supports, or gives information about, the main idea.

2 If you are trying to figure out the order of sentences in a paragraph, look for signal words (such as *first, then, last, later, finally*). Read the different sentence orders to yourself. Then choose the order that makes the most sense — or forms the most logical sequence.

 Go for it

Test Practice 5: Writing Paragraphs   Time: 8 minutes

Directions: Read the paragraph and answer the question that follows.

1.   American pioneers had difficult lives. They lived
in small, uncomfortable cabins. They suffered from
many diseases. _____

Which sentence best fills the blank in the paragraph?

Ⓐ The early pioneers came to America from Europe.

Ⓑ Native Americans introduced new foods to the pioneers.

Ⓒ A large number of pioneer women knew how to read.

Ⓓ Pioneer families had to grow or catch all their own food.

2.   Interesting names are used to describe kangaroos.
The most important male kangaroo in a group is called
a Boomer. _____ A baby kangaroo is known as a Joey.

Ⓐ A mother is called a Blue Flyer.

Ⓑ The baby is only a few inches long when it is born.

Ⓒ Kangaroos have powerful back legs.

Ⓓ Kangaroos live together in large groups.

3.   Some of the planets that travel around our sun are
called "gas giants." They are called *giants* because they
are very large. They are called *gas* giants because they
are made mostly of gas, rather than rock. _____

Ⓐ The earth is a small, rocky planet.

Ⓑ Uranus is one of the gas giants.

Ⓒ Nine planets travel around our sun.

Ⓓ In fairy tales, giants are huge creatures.

4.   Sailors use special words for directions. _____
The front of a ship is the "fore." The back of the ship is the "aft."

Ⓐ "Starboard" means right, and "port" means left.

Ⓑ The rudder, which steers the ship, is located in the back.

Ⓒ A dinghy is a small boat.

Ⓓ In the past, sailors used the stars to figure out what direction
they were traveling.

5. ¹Morton began telling everybody that they could save the soil by planting more trees.

   ²Because of Morton, the state government of Nebraska set aside one day a year especially for tree planting.

   ³In the late 1800s, a Nebraskan named J. Sterling Morton noticed that there were not enough trees in his state.

   ⁴Because of the lack of trees, the soil was drying up and blowing away in many places.

   In which order would the sentences make the best paragraph?

   Ⓐ 3 - 4 - 1 - 2   Ⓒ 1 - 2 - 3 - 4
   Ⓑ 4 - 1 - 2 - 3   Ⓓ 2 - 3 - 4 - 1

6. ¹At the end of the trail a tiny snail was inching slowly along.

   ²When Ahmed went to bed on Monday night, it was raining hard.

   ³On the sidewalk, he noticed a long silver trail.

   ⁴Tuesday morning, Ahmed walked out of the front door and down the sidewalk on his way to the bus stop.

   In which order would the sentences make the best paragraph?

   Ⓐ 4 - 3 - 1 - 2   Ⓒ 2 - 4 - 3 - 1
   Ⓑ 2 - 3 - 1 - 4   Ⓓ 4 - 2 - 1 - 3

7. ¹Next, heat and stir the milk until it begins to boil.

   ²Add the hot milk slowly to the beaten eggs and return the mixture to the stove.

   ³Stir the milk and egg mixture until it begins to thicken; then take the pudding off the stove and add vanilla.

   ⁴To make vanilla pudding, begin by getting out milk, sugar, eggs, and vanilla.

   In which order would the sentences make the best paragraph?

   Ⓐ 2 - 1 - 3 - 4   Ⓒ 1 - 4 - 2 - 3
   Ⓑ 4 - 3 - 1 - 2   Ⓓ 4 - 1 - 2 - 3

8. ¹In 1924, he was elected President of the United States.

   ²He went to college in Amherst, Massachusetts.

   ³Calvin Coolidge was born in Plymouth, Vermont.

   ⁴In 1919, he became the governor of Massachusetts.

   In which order would the sentences make the best paragraph?

   Ⓐ 4 - 1 - 3 - 2   Ⓒ 3 - 2 - 4 - 1
   Ⓑ 2 - 1 - 3 - 4   Ⓓ 1 - 2 - 3 - 4

STOP

Number Correct/Total = _____ /8

Spelling

Recognizing correct spelling

Directions: Choose the word that is spelled correctly.

A Yoko _____ the cave.

- Ⓐ exsplored
- Ⓑ explorred
- Ⓒ eksplored
- Ⓓ explored

Directions: Read the phrases. In one of the phrases, the underlined word is spelled incorrectly for the way it is used. Choose the phrase in which the underlined word is NOT spelled correctly.

B Ⓐ hit the <u>bawl</u>
  Ⓑ two red <u>roses</u>
  Ⓒ <u>bare</u> feet
  Ⓓ <u>heal</u> the sick dog

Example A asks you to pick the correct spelling of a word. Choice Ⓓ, *explored*, is correct. The other choices show common spelling errors.

Example B tests your knowledge of words that sound alike but are spelled differently. These words are called **homonyms**, or **homophones**.

Each underlined word in Example B is a real word, but one of them is spelled incorrectly for the way it is used. In choice Ⓐ, the phrase should say *hit the ball*, not the *bawl*. Choice Ⓐ is the answer.

Hint

To be a better speller, use your dictionary whenever you are not sure how to spell a word.

Test-Taking Tips

1 First, eliminate the answers you *know* are misspelled. If you are not sure how a word is spelled, look for the answer choice you think you have seen before.

2 Always read directions carefully. Be alert for items such as Example B, where you are supposed to find the word that is NOT spelled correctly.

3 When presented with homonyms, as in Example B, be sure to read each phrase carefully. The other words in the phrase will give you context clues that tell you which spelling should be used.

Go for i

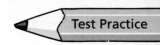

Test Practice 6: Spelling

Time: **20** minutes

Questions 1–15. Choose the word that is spelled correctly.

1. The _____ closes at 10:00.

   Ⓐ resterant
   Ⓑ resteraunt
   Ⓒ restaraunt
   Ⓓ restaurant

2. It takes _____ to open this jar.

   Ⓐ strength
   Ⓑ strenth
   Ⓒ stregth
   Ⓓ strenghth

3. The actress gave a loud _____.

   Ⓐ shreek
   Ⓑ shreak
   Ⓒ shreik
   Ⓓ shriek

4. Smoke poured out of the _____.

   Ⓐ chimny
   Ⓑ chimnee
   Ⓒ chimney
   Ⓓ chimey

5. Lace is very _____.

   Ⓐ delicate
   Ⓑ delacite
   Ⓒ delicite
   Ⓓ dellicate

6. For an _____, dial 911.

   Ⓐ emerjency
   Ⓑ emergency
   Ⓒ emerjincy
   Ⓓ emergincy

7. Joni was _____.

   Ⓐ dissapointed
   Ⓑ disapointed
   Ⓒ dissappointed
   Ⓓ disappointed

8. A _____ was nibbling leaves.

   Ⓐ geraffe
   Ⓑ giraffe
   Ⓒ gerafe
   Ⓓ giraff

9. Living near your school is _____.

   Ⓐ convenent
   Ⓑ cunvenient
   Ⓒ convenient
   Ⓓ conveniant

10. The dog dashed after a _____.

    Ⓐ squirl
    Ⓑ squirrel
    Ⓒ squirle
    Ⓓ squirrl

11. How much _____ is in your pocket?

    Ⓐ monie
    Ⓑ mony
    Ⓒ moniy
    Ⓓ money

12. The _____ of the room is ten feet.

    Ⓐ height
    Ⓑ heighth
    Ⓒ hieght
    Ⓓ hight

13. Use the _____ cleaner.

    Ⓐ vacume
    Ⓑ vacum
    Ⓒ vacoum
    Ⓓ vacuum

14. Put some _____ on the salad.

    Ⓐ vinegar
    Ⓑ vinegor
    Ⓒ vineger
    Ⓓ vinnegar

15. This letter is from the _____.

    Ⓐ govermint
    Ⓑ goverment
    Ⓒ government
    Ⓓ gouverment

GO ON

77

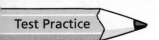

Questions 16–25. Read the phrases. In one of the phrases, the underlined word is spelled incorrectly for the way it is used. Choose the phrase in which the underlined word is NOT spelled correctly.

16. (A) break the cup

    (B) go threw the tunnel

    (C) a knight in armor

    (D) the rays of the sun

17. (A) pull on the reins

    (B) knead the bread

    (C) a dough and her fawn

    (D) tow a car

18. (A) a scene in a play

    (B) a not in the rope

    (C) wings of the fairy

    (D) down in the cellar

19. (A) fly the plain

    (B) a herd of cattle

    (C) go past the stop sign

    (D) feeling bored

20. (A) run over there

    (B) knows my name

    (C) lift the heavy wait

    (D) a fishing pole

21. (A) dig through the sand

    (B) a bail of hay

    (C) bury the bone

    (D) bare feet

22. (A) foot on the brake

    (B) buy a book

    (C) a loaf of bred

    (D) hear the song

23. (A) stay at the inn

    (B) dye her hair red

    (C) my dear friend

    (D) nun of the toys

24. (A) a pare of shoes

    (B) mowed the grass

    (C) a yellow flower

    (D) missed the boat

25. (A) the fourth stair

    (B) the hole pie

    (C) led the way

    (D) a guest for dinner

Number Correct/Total = _____ /25

Punctuation

Using correct punctuation in sentences and letters

Directions: Read each sentence. Choose the word or words that best fit the blank.

A We ate dinner at _____.

    Ⓐ six o,clock

    Ⓑ six oclock'

    Ⓒ six' oclock

    Ⓓ six o'clock

Directions: Read the sentence. Choose the correct way to write the underlined part.

B Martina <u>shouted Watch out!</u>

    Ⓐ shouted, "Watch out!"

    Ⓑ "shouted Watch out!"

    Ⓒ shouted, "Watch out!

    Ⓓ shouted "Watch out!"

For Example A, the correct answer is choice Ⓓ. The word *o'clock* is always punctuated with an apostrophe (') after the first *o*. For Example B, choice Ⓐ is correct. There should be a comma after *shouted*, and there should be quotation marks before *Watch* and after the exclamation mark. The other choices either leave out punctuation marks or put them in the wrong place.

In these examples, you are told which part of the sentence you must punctuate correctly.

Now let's look at a different type of question.

Directions: Read the sentences. Find the sentence that shows correct punctuation.

C Ⓐ "Good morning, students," said the store manager.

    Ⓑ "Welcome to the Food Mart of Oakville Ohio."

    Ⓒ "We will show you how we order shelve and sell food."

    Ⓓ "Does anybody have any questions."

In this example, you must look at four different sentences to find the one that is correct. The correct answer to Example C is choice Ⓐ. Choice Ⓑ is wrong because there is no comma between *Oakville* and *Ohio*. Choice Ⓒ is wrong because there should be a comma after *order* and after *shelve*. Choice Ⓓ is wrong because the sentence is a question and should end with a question mark.

Language Rules

Every sentence needs a **punctuation mark** at the end.

► Use a period, question mark, or exclamation mark, depending on the type of sentence.

It is raining outside.
How I hate rainy days!
Will it be sunny tomorrow?

Use a **period** —

► after an abbreviation

Mr. Bates, Nov. 12

► after a person's initials

Peter J. Morales

Use a **comma** —

► between a city and a state

Fairbanks, Alaska

► in dates, between the day and year

April 1, 1988

► in friendly letters, after the salutation and after the closing

Dear Ashley,
Forever yours,

► to separate words in a series

The playground has swings, slides, and seesaws.

► to set off certain words and phrases at the beginning of a sentence and in direct address

Once upon a time,
Scamp, fetch the stick.

► before a quotation

Ms. Biko said, "Quiet down."

Use **apostrophes** —

► in contractions

can't   I'm   he'd

► to show ownership

the officer's badge

Use **quotation marks** when telling the exact words someone says or said.

Mom cried, "No muddy feet on the couch!"

Test-Taking Tips

1 Look at every punctuation mark. Is a punctuation mark needed there? If so, is the correct mark used?

2 Read each sentence to yourself to see if it sounds right. Wherever you pause in the sentence, there should be a punctuation mark.

3 Look for sentences with missing punctuation.

Go for it

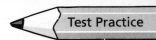

Test Practice 7 : Punctuation

Time: **14** minutes

Questions 1–6. Read each sentence. Choose the word
or words that best fit the blank.

1. After swimming, Jared _____ shake
   the water from his ear.

   Ⓐ couldnt
   Ⓑ couldn't
   Ⓒ could'nt
   Ⓓ couldnt'

2. Henri rode the bus to _____.

   Ⓐ Baltimore, Maryland
   Ⓑ Baltimore. Maryland
   Ⓒ Baltimore' Maryland
   Ⓓ Baltimore Maryland

3. _____ Jo Beth walked downstairs
   while fast asleep.

   Ⓐ The other night
   Ⓑ The other night.
   Ⓒ The other night,
   Ⓓ The other night?

4. The Mertzes took _____ to the
   picnic.

   Ⓐ salad, sandwiches and juice
   Ⓑ salad, sandwiches, and juice
   Ⓒ salad sandwiches, and juice
   Ⓓ salad sandwiches and juice

5. Has anybody seen the _____

   Ⓐ tennis rackets.
   Ⓑ tennis rackets"
   Ⓒ tennis rackets!
   Ⓓ tennis rackets?

6. _____ looked at the rash on Karl's
   elbow.

   Ⓐ Dr. Singh
   Ⓑ Dr, Singh
   Ⓒ Dr' Singh
   Ⓓ Dr Singh

Questions 7–10. Read the sentence. Choose the correct way to
write the underlined part.

7. <u>Kevin get</u> the tire pump.

   Ⓐ Kevin. get
   Ⓑ Kevin get
   Ⓒ Kevin' get
   Ⓓ Kevin, get

8. Maria <u>whispered There's</u> a deer over
   there."

   Ⓐ whispered, "There's
   Ⓑ whispered "There's
   Ⓒ whispered, There's
   Ⓓ whispered ",There's

9. The <u>cats eyes</u> glowed brightly.

   Ⓐ cats eyes
   Ⓑ cats eyes'
   Ⓒ cats' eyes'
   Ⓓ cat's eyes

10. The letter was dated <u>Nov 20</u>.

   Ⓐ Nov, 20
   Ⓑ Nov 20
   Ⓒ Nov. 20
   Ⓓ Nov' 20

Questions 11–14. Read the sentences. Find the sentence that shows correct punctuation.

11. Ⓐ At noon yesterday, the mail carrier knocked at the door.
    Ⓑ She had a letter addressed to C L Cispes.
    Ⓒ The letter had been mailed from Milwaukee Wisconsin.
    Ⓓ It was dated July 29 1990.

12. Ⓐ Dr. Babbitt turned on the television news.
    Ⓑ The announcer said, And now some news about the quake."
    Ⓒ A map of Portland Maine flashed on the screen.
    Ⓓ He said "Today a small earthquake shook Portland."

13. Ⓐ Last night a firefly got into my room?
    Ⓑ How pretty it looked as it flew around in the dark!
    Ⓒ The next morning I couldnt find it anywhere.
    Ⓓ Do you think it flew out the window.

14. Ⓐ Darnell cant understand why everybody likes ice cream.
    Ⓑ He dislikes vanilla chocolate and strawberry.
    Ⓒ Hed rather snack on some peanuts or fruit.
    Ⓓ He says, "Ice cream tastes like baby food to me!"

Questions 15–16. Read the letter. Choose the correct way to write the underlined parts.

February 6, 1990

Dear Melanie
———
15

    I am writing you a letter because I haven't been able to reach you by telephone. Where have you been? My dad says he'll take us skating on Saturday morning. Let me know if you want to come.

Your friend
———
16
Mei Su

15. Ⓐ Dear Melanie
    Ⓑ Dear, Melanie
    Ⓒ Dear Melanie.
    Ⓓ Dear Melanie,

16. Ⓐ Your friend.
    Ⓑ Your friend,
    Ⓒ "Your friend"
    Ⓓ Your friend

Number Correct/Total = _____ /16

Capitalization

Using correct capitalization in sentences and letters

Directions: Read each sentence. Find the answer that best fits the blank.

A We read _____ last month.

Ⓐ *Charlotte's web*

Ⓑ *charlotte's web*

Ⓒ *Charlotte's Web*

Ⓓ *charlotte's Web*

Directions: Read the sentences. Choose the one that uses correct capitalization.

B Ⓐ Cousin Billie works for First national bank.

Ⓑ His office is in the center of Brentville.

Ⓒ The bank is right across from central square park.

Ⓓ Often i meet him for lunch.

In Example A, the correct answer is choice Ⓒ because every important word in a book title should be capitalized. In Example B, choice Ⓑ is correct because the name of a city should be capitalized. Choice Ⓐ is wrong because the important words in a business name should be capitalized. Choice Ⓒ is wrong because the name of the park should be capitalized. Choice Ⓓ is wrong because the pronoun *I* should be capitalized.

Language Rules

▶ Capitalize "firsts"—the first word in a sentence, in a quotation, in the salutation and closing of a letter.

> He said, "Come on in."
> Dear Judith,
> Love always,

▶ Capitalize the names, initials, and titles of persons and places.

> Dr. C.G. Cucci
> Central Park

▶ Capitalize the pronoun *I*, days, holidays, months, and proper adjectives.

> Wednesday, June 7
> an American citizen

Test-Taking Tips

1 Don't be fooled by answer choices that look almost exactly the same. Check each answer choice carefully, looking for errors in capitalization.

2 If you are not sure of the answer, choose the one with the most capital letters. It will usually—but not always—be the correct choice.

Go for it

Test Practice 8: Capitalization

Time: **14** minutes

Questions 1–10. Read each sentence. Find the answer that best fits the blank.

1. The principal introduced _____.

   Ⓐ senator dowd
   Ⓑ senator Dowd
   Ⓒ Senator dowd
   Ⓓ Senator Dowd

2. The airplane had to land in _____.

   Ⓐ Chicago, illinois
   Ⓑ Chicago, Illinois
   Ⓒ chicago, illinois
   Ⓓ chicago, Illinois

3. Mrs. Brady's class saw the play _____.

   Ⓐ *Night Of Danger*
   Ⓑ *night of danger*
   Ⓒ *Night of Danger*
   Ⓓ *Night of danger*

4. Mom signed the check _____.

   Ⓐ Joanna j. Lembesis
   Ⓑ joanna j. Lembesis
   Ⓒ Joanna J. Lembesis
   Ⓓ joanna j. lembesis

5. We saw some dinosaur bones at the _____.

   Ⓐ Museum of Natural History
   Ⓑ Museum of natural history
   Ⓒ Museum Of Natural History
   Ⓓ museum of natural history

6. The floors were made of _____.

   Ⓐ Italian marble
   Ⓑ italian Marble
   Ⓒ Italian Marble
   Ⓓ italian marble

7. The kids shouted, _____.

   Ⓐ "trick or treat!"
   Ⓑ "Trick Or Treat!"
   Ⓒ "trick or Treat!"
   Ⓓ "Trick or treat!"

8. The boat sailed to _____.

   Ⓐ Australia and africa
   Ⓑ australia and africa
   Ⓒ Australia and Africa
   Ⓓ australia and Africa

9. Our family usually celebrates _____.

   Ⓐ Thanksgiving in boston
   Ⓑ Thanksgiving in Boston
   Ⓒ thanksgiving in boston
   Ⓓ thanksgiving in Boston

10. Many people visit the ____ each year.

    Ⓐ statue of liberty
    Ⓑ Statue of liberty
    Ⓒ Statue Of Liberty
    Ⓓ Statue of Liberty

GO ON

Questions 11–14. Read the sentences. Find the one that is capitalized correctly.

11. Ⓐ I love going to the Mill creek library.
    Ⓑ The children's librarian is Ms. Hadjian.
    Ⓒ She suggested a book called *Pippi longstocking*.
    Ⓓ I took it home monday and finished it tuesday.

12. Ⓐ For emily's birthday, her mom took us to the mall.
    Ⓑ Emily went to a store called Doll heaven.
    Ⓒ She picked out a german doll with long braids.
    Ⓓ Then we went to the movie, *Goblins, Part Three*.

13. Ⓐ Many people think February is a cold, unpleasant month.
    Ⓑ i disagree with them.
    Ⓒ It is a great month because it has valentine's day.
    Ⓓ I buy all my holiday cards at dove's card shop.

14. Ⓐ yesterday we had a fire drill at school.
    Ⓑ When the bell rang, i jumped out of my seat.
    Ⓒ Our teacher said, "Form a line and don't talk."
    Ⓓ Out on the playground, mr. Mahoney counted us.

Questions 15–16. Read the letter. Choose the correct way to write the underlined parts.

December 14, 1990

dear mayor gibbs,
_____
15

    Thank you for the new park on Center Street. My friends and I play there every weekend. It is a great park. Could you come play stickball with us sometime?

yours truly
_____
16
everett wilson

15. Ⓐ Dear Mayor Gibbs,
    Ⓑ Dear mayor Gibbs,
    Ⓒ dear Mayor Gibbs,
    Ⓓ Dear Mayor gibbs,

16. Ⓐ Yours Truly,
    Ⓑ yours truly,
    Ⓒ Yours truly,
    Ⓓ yours Truly,

Number Correct/Total = _____ /16

85

Research Skills

Classifying information and using alphabetical order

Directions: Read the words. Which word comes first in alphabetical order?

A Ⓐ crowd   Ⓒ curious

    Ⓑ chocolate   Ⓓ center

Choice Ⓓ is correct; *center* comes first in alphabetical order.

Now let's look at a different kind of question.

Directions: Read each group of words. Which of these words could be main headings that include the other three words?

B Ⓐ dress   **C** Ⓐ daisy

    Ⓑ pants   Ⓑ rose

    Ⓒ shirt   Ⓒ flower

    Ⓓ clothing   Ⓓ lily

In Example B, choices Ⓐ, Ⓑ, and Ⓒ are all types of clothing: *dress, pants, shirt*. So the correct answer is choice Ⓓ, *clothing*, because it could be the main heading that includes the other three. In Example C, choice Ⓒ, *flower*, is correct because each of the other three is a type of flower.

Test-Taking Tips

1 To find which word comes first in alphabetical order, look at the first letter of each word. Find the word that starts with the letter closest to the beginning of the alphabet. (*Apple* comes before *cat*.)

2 If all the words in a list begin with the same letter, look at the second letter (as in Example A). If the second letters are all the same (as in *back, ball, banana, basket*), look at the third letter.

3 To find the main heading, look at all four words in a list and decide what they have in common. Three of them will be specific examples of something, such as kinds of clothing or kinds of flowers. One answer choice will be a general word. It is the heading that includes the other three.

Go for it

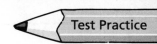
Test Practice ⑨: Research Skills

Time: **10** minutes

Questions 1–7. Read each group of words. Which word comes first in alphabetical order?

1. Ⓐ magician
   Ⓑ ordinary
   Ⓒ northern
   Ⓓ package

2. Ⓐ graceful
   Ⓑ glue
   Ⓒ giggle
   Ⓓ ghost

3. Ⓐ column
   Ⓑ connect
   Ⓒ countless
   Ⓓ compare

4. Ⓐ slick
   Ⓑ slap
   Ⓒ sloppy
   Ⓓ slug

5. Ⓐ ugly
   Ⓑ valley
   Ⓒ toothpick
   Ⓓ warrior

6. Ⓐ dune
   Ⓑ dim
   Ⓒ droop
   Ⓓ delight

7. Ⓐ jewel
   Ⓑ jest
   Ⓒ jelly
   Ⓓ jetty

Questions 8–14. Read each group of words. Which word could be a main heading that includes the other three?

8. Ⓐ milk
   Ⓑ juice
   Ⓒ drink
   Ⓓ water

9. Ⓐ frown
   Ⓑ smile
   Ⓒ wink
   Ⓓ expression

10. Ⓐ room
    Ⓑ kitchen
    Ⓒ den
    Ⓓ bedroom

11. Ⓐ joint
    Ⓑ shoulder
    Ⓒ elbow
    Ⓓ knee

12. Ⓐ oak
    Ⓑ tree
    Ⓒ maple
    Ⓓ pine

13. Ⓐ carrot
    Ⓑ celery
    Ⓒ potato
    Ⓓ vegetable

14. Ⓐ jump
    Ⓑ twirl
    Ⓒ throw
    Ⓓ movement

Number Correct/Total = _____ /14

Reference Sources

Locating information in reference sources
and parts of books

Directions: Use this sample index to answer the question.

INDEX
ants, 10–11
badgers, 22–24
chalky soil, 7
clay, 8
earthworms, 16–17
ground beetles, 18
foxes, 27–29

A If you want to find information on foxes, you should look on pages —

Ⓐ 10–11

Ⓑ 16–17

Ⓒ 22–24

Ⓓ 27–29

For Example A, choice Ⓓ is correct because information about foxes can be found on pages 27-29. This kind of question asks you to use information given in an **index** or **table of contents**. These are parts of a book. Other kinds of test questions may ask you to find information in a sample page from a dictionary. Some test questions ask you to choose the best book to look in for certain information.

B To find information on farming in Mexico, you should look in —

Ⓐ a dictionary   Ⓒ an atlas

Ⓑ an encyclopedia   Ⓓ a telephone book

For Example B, choice Ⓑ is correct. You would find information about farming in Mexico in an **encyclopedia**. An enyclopedia is a large reference book, or set of reference books, that contains articles giving factual information on many specific topics. A **dictionary** is a book of words and their meanings. An **atlas** is a book of maps. A **telephone directory** lists people's names, addresses, and telephone numbers.

Test-Taking Tips

1 To find what chapter contains certain information, look in a table of contents. To find what pages have certain facts, use the index.

2 Look for key words in the question. (In Example A, the key word is *foxes*. In Example B, the key words are *farming in Mexico*.) The key words will help you decide where to find the information.

Go for it

Test Practice 10 : Reference Sources   Time: **12** minutes

Questions 1–5. Use the sample table of contents and index to answer each question.

CONTENTS

INDEX

1. In which chapter would you find information about blocks?

   Ⓐ Chapter 1
   Ⓑ Chapter 2
   Ⓒ Chapter 3
   Ⓓ Chapter 4

2. In which chapter would you find information about games with marbles?

   Ⓐ Chapter 2
   Ⓑ Chapter 3
   Ⓒ Chapter 4
   Ⓓ Chapter 5

3. In which chapter would you find information about teddy bears?

   Ⓐ Chapter 1
   Ⓑ Chapter 2
   Ⓒ Chapter 4
   Ⓓ Chapter 5

4. On which page would you find information about talking dolls?

   Ⓐ page 12
   Ⓑ page 17
   Ⓒ page 18
   Ⓓ page 22

5. To which pages should you turn to read about plastic blocks?

   Ⓐ pages 38-49
   Ⓑ pages 38-42
   Ⓒ pages 43-46
   Ⓓ pages 47-49

GO ON

Questions 6–8. Use the sample dictionary entries to answer each question.

> **croc·o·dile** [krŏk′ ə dīl] *n.* a large animal that looks like a lizard and lives in water.
>
> **cro·ny** [krō′ nē] *n.* a close friend; pal
>
> **crop** [krŏp] *n.* 1. a plant grown for use. 2. a short haircut. 3. a pouch in a bird's throat. 4. a short whip.
>
> **cro·quet** [krō kā′] *n.* a game in which players hit balls through hoops.

6. A *crony* is a —

   Ⓐ large animal

   Ⓑ game

   Ⓒ kind of plant

   Ⓓ close friend

7. Which definition of *crop* best fits the way the word is used in the sentence below?

   The farmer complained that the wheat *crop* was small this year.

   Ⓐ 1   Ⓒ 3
   Ⓑ 2   Ⓓ 4

8. Which word is spelled correctly?

   Ⓐ crokodile   Ⓒ krony
   Ⓑ krop   Ⓓ croquet

Questions 9–12. Choose the best answer to each question.

---

9. To find a list of pet stores near your home, you should look in —

   Ⓐ an encyclopedia

   Ⓑ a telephone book

   Ⓒ a dictionary

   Ⓓ an atlas

10. To find out how to pronounce the word *cyclops*, you should look in —

    Ⓐ an encyclopedia

    Ⓑ a telephone book

    Ⓒ a dictionary

    Ⓓ an atlas

11. Where should you look to learn about the Revolutionary War?

    Ⓐ encyclopedia

    Ⓑ telephone book

    Ⓒ dictionary

    Ⓓ atlas

12. To find out where the Missouri River is, you should look in —

    Ⓐ an encyclopedia

    Ⓑ a telephone book

    Ⓒ a dictionary

    Ⓓ an atlas

Number Correct/Total = _____ /12

Maps, Charts, and Graphs

Reading and interpreting graphic aids

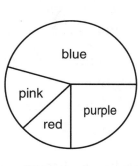

Directions: Use the map to answer the question.

		School	
	Point St.	Washington St.	Canal St.
		Main Street	

A On which street is the school?

Ⓐ Main Street
Ⓑ Little Point Street
Ⓒ Canal Street
Ⓓ Washington Street

If you study the map, you can see that the school is on Washington Street. The correct answer is choice Ⓓ. A **map** gives information about places in picture form. A **circle graph** gives other kinds of information in picture form. (This is sometimes called a **pie graph** because it looks like a pie with slices.) Use the circle graph to answer the question below.

B The greatest number of bicycles are —

Ⓐ pink
Ⓑ red
Ⓒ blue
Ⓓ purple

The circle graph shows how the bicycles are divided by color. By studying the graph, you can see that the biggest "slice of the pie" is labeled *blue*. The correct answer is choice Ⓒ.

Other test questions may ask you to read a **table** of numbers or a **schedule**.

Test-Taking Tips

1 Look at the map, graph, or table first to see what kind of information it shows. Then read each question carefully and look back at the map, graph, or table to find the answer.

2 Look for key words and phrases to answer each question. (In Example B, the key word is *greatest*.)

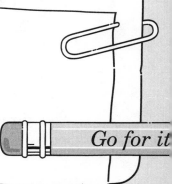

Go for it

Test Practice 11: Maps, Charts, and Graphs   Time: 10 minutes

Questions 1–6. Use the map to answer each question.

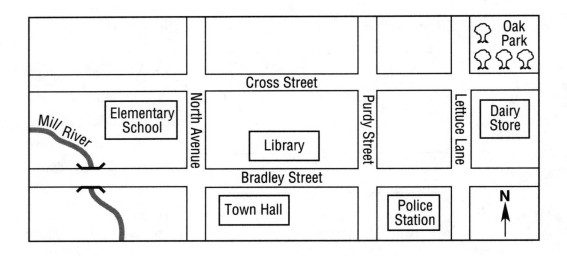

1. Which street crosses the Mill River?

   Ⓐ Cross Street
   Ⓑ North Avenue
   Ⓒ Bradley Street
   Ⓓ Lettuce Lane

2. Which building is at the corner of Purdy Street and Bradley Street?

   Ⓐ the town hall
   Ⓑ the police station
   Ⓒ the library
   Ⓓ the dairy store

3. Oak Park is at the corner of Cross Street and —

   Ⓐ Purdy Street
   Ⓑ North Avenue
   Ⓒ Lettuce Lane
   Ⓓ Bradley Street

4. If you leave the town hall and travel north on North Avenue, you will come to the —

   Ⓐ elementary school
   Ⓑ library
   Ⓒ police station
   Ⓓ dairy store

5. What is directly across the street from Oak Park?

   Ⓐ the library
   Ⓑ the elementary school
   Ⓒ the dairy store
   Ⓓ the town hall

6. To get from the town hall to Lettuce Lane, you have to cross —

   Ⓐ the Mill River
   Ⓑ North Avenue
   Ⓒ Cross Street
   Ⓓ Purdy Street

 GO ON

Questions 7–9. Use the schedule to answer each question.

Questions 10–12. Use the circle graph to answer each question.

FIELD DAY SCHEDULE		
Event	**Time**	**Place**
High jump	10:00 A.M.	Lonzak Field
Broad jump	10:30 A.M.	Lonzak Field
Softball	10:00 A.M.	Martin Field
Races	11:00 A.M.	Lonzak Field
Soccer	1:00 P.M.	Martin Field
Double Dutch	9:30 A.M.	School Gym

WHAT CHILDREN ATE AT THE PICNIC

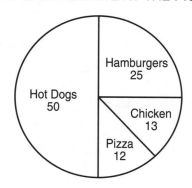

7. What event will take place at 10:30 A.M. at Lonzak Field?

    Ⓐ Races

    Ⓑ High jump

    Ⓒ Double Dutch

    Ⓓ Broad jump

8. When and where will the softball game take place?

    Ⓐ 10:00 A.M. at Lonzak Field

    Ⓑ 10:00 A.M. at Martin Field

    Ⓒ 1:00 P.M. at Martin Field

    Ⓓ 1:00 P.M. in the gym

9. What is the first event of the day?

    Ⓐ High jump

    Ⓑ Softball

    Ⓒ Double Dutch

    Ⓓ Soccer

10. How many children had chicken at the picnic?

    Ⓐ 12

    Ⓑ 13

    Ⓒ 25

    Ⓓ 50

11. Which food was most popular at the picnic?

    Ⓐ hot dogs

    Ⓑ hamburgers

    Ⓒ pizza

    Ⓓ chicken

12. Which food was least popular?

    Ⓐ hot dogs

    Ⓑ hamburgers

    Ⓒ pizza

    Ⓓ chicken

Number Correct/Total = _____ /12

*This test will tell you how well you might score on a standardized language arts test **after** using this book. If you compare your scores on Tryout Tests 1 and 2, you'll see how much you've learned!*

Language Arts Tryout Test 2

Time: **30** minutes

Directions: Follow the directions for each part of the test. Read each question carefully and fill in the circle beside the answer you choose. The answer to the sample question (**S**) has been filled in for you.

Questions 1–5. Choose the word or group of words that best completes the sentence.

S Last month Cheryl _____ her dad in Honolulu.

Ⓐ visit

Ⓑ will visit

● visited

Ⓓ visiting

1. The telephone rang _____ in the empty house.

Ⓐ shrilly

Ⓑ shrill

Ⓒ shriller

Ⓓ shrillest

2. _____ wrote messages in secret code.

Ⓐ Him and I

Ⓑ He and I

Ⓒ Me and him

Ⓓ I and he

3. A stork _____ in the river, looking for fish.

Ⓐ stand

Ⓑ have stood

Ⓒ do stand

Ⓓ stands

4. Of all the students in the class, Ana is the _____.

Ⓐ friendlier

Ⓑ friendly

Ⓒ most friendliest

Ⓓ friendliest

5. Jeff insisted that the bike was _____.

Ⓐ his

Ⓑ him

Ⓒ he's

Ⓓ himself

Questions 6–7. Choose the simple subject of the sentence.

6. Uncle Kevin painted his sportscar red and purple.
       Ⓐ   Ⓑ   Ⓒ   Ⓓ

7. After the game, everybody went swimming to cool off.
       Ⓐ   Ⓑ   Ⓒ   Ⓓ

GO ON ➤

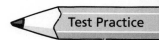

Questions 8–9. Choose the simple predicate of the sentence.

8. Eunice discovered the missing puzzle piece under the sofa.
    Ⓐ   Ⓑ   Ⓒ   Ⓓ

9. The magician cleverly concealed a live rabbit!
      Ⓐ   Ⓑ   Ⓒ   Ⓓ

Questions 10–11. Read the four groups of words. Choose the one that is
a correct sentence.

10. Ⓐ Dylan climbed the tree he was really high up.
 Ⓑ Called his mother to see where he was.
 Ⓒ His mother was impressed she went to get the camera.
 Ⓓ In the picture, Dylan is hidden by the leaves!

11. Ⓐ Today the tomato a popular vegetable everywhere.
 Ⓑ Some people used to think tomatoes were poisonous.
 Ⓒ There are many kinds of tomatoes some are purple.
 Ⓓ Disagree whether they are a fruit or a vegetable.

Questions 12–13. Read the underlined sentences. Choose the answer that
best combines them into one clear sentence without changing their meaning.

12. A car raced down the street.
 The car was noisy.

 Ⓐ A car raced down the noisy street.
 Ⓑ A noisy car raced down the street.
 Ⓒ A car it was noisy raced down the street.
 Ⓓ A car raced down the street and it was noisy.

13. Leon made some lemonade.
 Leon sold the lemonade.

 Ⓐ Leon made some lemonade and sold it.
 Ⓑ Leon made lemonade and sold lemonade.
 Ⓒ Leon made lemonade and sold.
 Ⓓ The lemonade made Leon and sold it.

Language Arts Tryout Test 2 (continued)

Questions 14–15. Read the paragraph and answer the question.

14.   Fire ants first arrived in the United States from South America about fifty years ago. They live in the southern states but are beginning to move north. Fire ants cause a lot of damage. _____

Which sentence best fits in the paragraph?

Ⓐ There are many different kinds of ants.

Ⓑ Fifty years ago, World War II was going on.

Ⓒ These ants destroy crops and sting people.

Ⓓ Each group of ants has a queen.

15. ¹Denzil got out wrapping paper, tape, scissors, and ribbon.
²Then he wrapped the gift and taped the paper.
³He tied a ribbon around the wrapped present.
⁴He cut a piece of paper big enough for the gift.

In which order would the sentences make the best paragraph?

Ⓐ 1 - 4 - 2 - 3   Ⓒ 1 - 2 - 4 - 3

Ⓑ 4 - 3 - 2 - 1   Ⓓ 1 - 3 - 4 - 2

Questions 16–19. Read the phrases. In one of the phrases, the underlined word is spelled incorrectly for the way it is used. Choose the phrase in which the underlined word is NOT spelled correctly.

16. Ⓐ <u>knead</u> some new shoes
    Ⓑ tie a <u>knot</u>
    Ⓒ <u>two</u> muffins
    Ⓓ <u>their</u> blue van

17. Ⓐ don't <u>tease</u>
    Ⓑ show me the <u>weigh</u>
    Ⓒ <u>some</u> of my friends
    Ⓓ the plant's <u>roots</u>

18. Ⓐ <u>brake</u> on the bicycle
    Ⓑ <u>wood</u> for the fireplace
    Ⓒ <u>so</u> the torn pants
    Ⓓ a sad <u>tale</u>

19. Ⓐ a <u>waist</u> of time
    Ⓑ <u>here</u> in the town
    Ⓒ <u>flew</u> over the trees
    Ⓓ the cat's <u>fur</u>

 GO ON

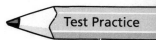

Questions 20–25. Read each sentence. Choose the sentence that has correct punctuation and capitalization.

20. Ⓐ Grandma works for the East Shore power company.
    Ⓑ Her job is to tell people how to save energy
    Ⓒ She visited my school on March 13, 1990.
    Ⓓ She said, "Students you can be energy-savers, too."

21. Ⓐ rena will take swimming lessons this summer.
    Ⓑ The lessons are at the Fifth Avenue Pool.
    Ⓒ They start july 2 and end August 15.
    Ⓓ The teachers name is Mrs. Edna S Symmons.

22. Ⓐ Mom said "I am taking vacation at home."
    Ⓑ She doesnt want to travel this year.
    Ⓒ She is tired of packing driving and worrying.
    Ⓓ She plans to sit and read novels at home.

23. Ⓐ Jill writes to a penpal in London england.
    Ⓑ The penpal's name is dr. Joyce Withers.
    Ⓒ She is thirty years older than Jill!
    Ⓓ Joyces letters are very amusing.

24. Ⓐ Juan, Carlos, and Mike hiked up the mountain.
    Ⓑ by the end of the day they were tired.
    Ⓒ Carlos said, I'll set up the tent.
    Ⓓ Juan and Mike made a fire and cooked irish stew.

25. Ⓐ mr. gregorian turned on the television.
    Ⓑ A smiling woman said, "buy orton's paper towels."
    Ⓒ "I don't want paper towels," answered Alex Gregorian.
    Ⓓ He turned off the tv picked up the paper and read.

Questions 26–29. Read and answer each question.

26. Which word comes first in alphabetical order?

    Ⓐ shawl

    Ⓑ slippery

    Ⓒ squeak

    Ⓓ separate

27. Which word is a main heading that includes the other three?

    Ⓐ tool

    Ⓑ drill

    Ⓒ hammer

    Ⓓ saw

 GO ON

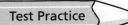

Language Arts Tryout Test 2 (continued)

28. If you want to find out how to pronounce the word *granite*, you should look in —

Ⓐ an atlas

Ⓑ a dictionary

Ⓒ an encyclopedia

Ⓓ a telephone book

29. Where should you look to find a sporting goods store in your area?

Ⓐ encyclopedia

Ⓑ atlas

Ⓒ dictionary

Ⓓ telephone book

Questions 30–31. Use the schedule to answer each question.

ACTIVITIES AT CAMP ROWE		
Time	**Weekdays**	**Saturday**
9:00 A.M.	Hike/Swim	Hike/Swim
10:00 A.M.	Crafts	Free Time
1:00 P.M.	Softball	Movie
3:00 P.M.	Riding	Riding
8:00 P.M.	Campfire	Campfire

30. What takes place at 10:00 A.M. on weekdays?

Ⓐ Hike/Swim   Ⓒ Free Time

Ⓑ Crafts   Ⓓ Softball

31. Which activity takes place only on Saturday?

Ⓐ Softball   Ⓒ Campfire

Ⓑ Riding   Ⓓ Movie

Questions 32–35. Use the sample dictionary entries to answer each question.

---

lim·er·ick [lǐm′ər ǐk] *n.* a five-line nonsense verse.

lim·pet [lǐm′pǐt] *n.* a brownish green saltwater shellfish.

line [līn] *n.* 1. a long, thin mark. 2. the border between two areas. 3. a row of people or things. 4. a short letter. 5. a telephone wire.

li·on [lī′ən] *n.* a large animal of the cat family which lives in Africa and parts of Asia.

---

32. A *limerick* is a kind of—

Ⓐ animal   Ⓒ wire

Ⓑ verse   Ⓓ shellfish

33. *Limpets* live in —

Ⓐ jungles   Ⓒ deserts

Ⓑ Africa   Ⓓ salt water

34. Which definition of *line* best fits the sentence below?

We crossed the *line* into Idaho.

Ⓐ 1   Ⓒ 3

Ⓑ 2   Ⓓ 4

35. Which word is spelled correctly?

Ⓐ limerik   Ⓒ limpet

Ⓑ lin   Ⓓ lian

Number Correct/Total = _____ /35

Top Ten Math Tips

1 Use scratch paper to write down the numbers you need to solve a problem.

2 Look for key words that tell you what kind of computation is needed, for example: *less than*, *greatest*, *between*, *nearest*, *least*, *closest*, and so on.

3 Try out *all* answer choices until you find the one that is correct. Sometimes the correct answer is *not given*. Then you should follow the directions for marking the Not Given choice (NG in this book).

4 Make sure you know what to solve for in each problem. Write a number sentence or an equation to help you solve it.

5 Write down each piece of information given in a problem, and write down or circle what each problem asks you to find. When you have an answer, go back and make sure it answers the question you wrote down or circled.

6 Rename fractions with different denominators as *like fractions* (with same denominators).

7 Always reduce fractions to their smallest parts. When looking for the correct answer to a problem with fractions, look for the one that has been reduced.

8 For a measurement or geometry problem, first write down the formula you need to solve the problem. Then "plug into" the formula the numbers from the problem.

9 Remember, an equation must stay balanced. What you do to one side of an equation you must do to the other side.

10 Check subtraction problems by adding; check division problems by multiplying; check multiplication by dividing.

*This test will tell you how well you might score on a standardized math test **before** using this book.*

Math Tryout Test 1

Time: **30** minutes

Directions: Find the best answer for each question. Fill in the circle for the answer you choose. If the correct answer is not given, choose NG. The answer to the sample question (**S**) has been filled in for you.

S Which is another name for 25?

- Ⓐ 5 tens and 2 ones
- ● 2 tens and 5 ones
- Ⓒ 1 tens and 5 ones
- Ⓓ 2 tens and 15 ones

1. Which numeral means three thousand, one hundred two?

- Ⓐ 3012
- Ⓑ 312
- Ⓒ 3120
- Ⓓ 3102

2. Which number statement is true?

- Ⓐ 610 > 806
- Ⓑ 608 < 610
- Ⓒ 601 > 608
- Ⓓ 806 < 610

3. What is another name for 2 hundreds and 4 tens?

- Ⓐ 20040
- Ⓑ 2004
- Ⓒ 240
- Ⓓ 204

4. Which number has the greatest value?

- Ⓐ 7213
- Ⓑ 7132
- Ⓒ 7321
- Ⓓ 7312

5. Which child is 5th in line?

Ⓐ   Ⓑ   Ⓒ   Ⓓ

6. Which number is one more than 189?

- Ⓐ 190
- Ⓑ 289
- Ⓒ 188
- Ⓓ 179

7. What is the value of the 4 in 8473?

- Ⓐ 4000
- Ⓑ 400
- Ⓒ 40
- Ⓓ 4

8. Look at the number pattern. What number comes next?

39, 42, 45, ___

- Ⓐ 46
- Ⓑ 47
- Ⓒ 48
- Ⓓ 49

GO ON

Math Tryout Test 1 (continued)

9. Which is another name for 922?

   Ⓐ 900 + 20 + 2

   Ⓑ 900 + 2 + 2

   Ⓒ 9 + 20 + 2

   Ⓓ 9 + 2 + 2

10. Which number is closest in value to

   $\boxed{39 - 21}$?

   Ⓐ 60

   Ⓑ 35

   Ⓒ 15

   Ⓓ 20

11. What fraction of the figure is shaded?

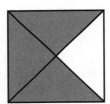

   Ⓐ $\frac{1}{4}$

   Ⓑ $\frac{4}{3}$

   Ⓒ $\frac{1}{3}$

   Ⓓ $\frac{3}{4}$

12. Which fraction is greater than $\frac{2}{3}$?

   Ⓐ $\frac{4}{5}$

   Ⓑ $\frac{2}{4}$

   Ⓒ $\frac{3}{6}$

   Ⓓ $\frac{1}{3}$

13. Which decimal has the least value?

   Ⓐ .200

   Ⓑ .020

   Ⓒ .002

   Ⓓ 2.00

14. Which number sentence shows how many fish there are all together?

   Ⓐ 8 − 4 = 4

   Ⓑ 2 + 4 = 6

   Ⓒ 4 − 2 = 2

   Ⓓ 4 × 2 = 8

15. What number fits in the box to complete this number sentence?

   $\boxed{10 \div 2 = \square}$

   Ⓐ 10

   Ⓑ 5

   Ⓒ 4

   Ⓓ 20

16. Which number sentence goes with

   $\boxed{11 + 5 = 16}$?

   Ⓐ 16 − 11 = 5

   Ⓑ 11 × 5 = 55

   Ⓒ 11 − 5 = 6

   Ⓓ 11 + 16 = 27

GO O

17. 623
   + 94

Ⓐ 617
Ⓑ 627
Ⓒ 717
Ⓓ 727
Ⓔ NG

18. 814
   − 372

Ⓐ 432
Ⓑ 442
Ⓒ 542
Ⓓ 582
Ⓔ NG

19. 43 × 4 =

Ⓐ 172
Ⓑ 167
Ⓒ 162
Ⓓ 152
Ⓔ NG

20. 6)78

Ⓐ 12
Ⓑ 13
Ⓒ 14
Ⓓ 23
Ⓔ NG

21. $6\frac{4}{5} - 1\frac{3}{5} =$

Ⓐ $6\frac{1}{5}$
Ⓑ 6
Ⓒ $5\frac{3}{5}$
Ⓓ $5\frac{2}{5}$
Ⓔ NG

22. $9.67
   + $4.99

Ⓐ $13.56
Ⓑ $13.66
Ⓒ $14.56
Ⓓ $14.66
Ⓔ $14.76

23. Rafe made 21 paintings for the art show. He sold 9 of them. How many did he have left?

Ⓐ 30
Ⓑ 12
Ⓒ 11
Ⓓ 9
Ⓔ NG

24. Three cans of soup cost $.99. How much do 5 cans cost?

Ⓐ $4.95
Ⓑ $1.98
Ⓒ $1.65
Ⓓ $1.32
Ⓔ NG

25. Shawna made 6 potholders in 3 days. Which number sentence can you use to find how many she made each day?

Ⓐ 6 ÷ 3 = ☐
Ⓑ 6 × 3 = ☐
Ⓒ 3 + ☐ = 6
Ⓓ ☐ − 6 = 3
Ⓔ NG

26. Sandy made $6.00 babysitting one day and $4.00 the next day. He also earned $2.00 pulling weeds. Then he spent half his money on a model car and the other half on a book. Which information is NOT needed to find how much Sandy spent on the model car?

Ⓐ He spent half his money on the model car.
Ⓑ He made $6.00 babysitting.
Ⓒ He made $4.00 babysitting.
Ⓓ He spent half his money on a book.
Ⓔ He made $2.00 pulling weeds.

Math Tryout Test 1 (continued)

27. Which figure is a rectangle?

Ⓐ

Ⓓ

Ⓑ

Ⓔ

Ⓒ

28. Which two figures have the same size and shape?

Ⓐ

Ⓓ

Ⓑ

Ⓔ

Ⓒ

29. What is the area of this shape?

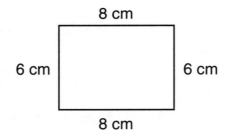

8 cm

6 cm   6 cm

8 cm

Ⓐ 14 cm²   Ⓓ 64 cm²

Ⓑ 28 cm²   Ⓔ NG

Ⓒ 48 cm²

30. What is the area of this figure in square units?

Ⓐ 15   Ⓓ 21

Ⓑ 16   Ⓔ NG

Ⓒ 17

31. Which figure can be folded along the line so that its parts exactly match?

Ⓐ   Ⓓ

Ⓑ   Ⓔ

Ⓒ

32. What time does the clock show?

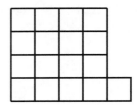

Ⓐ 7:45   Ⓓ 9:35

Ⓑ 7:55   Ⓔ NG

Ⓒ 9:25

GO ON

33. Andy and his uncle went fishing at 7:00. They came home 6 hours later. Which clock shows what time they got home?

Ⓐ Ⓒ Ⓑ Ⓓ

34. Which unit is best used to measure how much a package weighs?

Ⓐ pound

Ⓑ foot

Ⓒ inch

Ⓓ ton

35. How long is this piece of string?

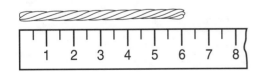

Ⓐ 5.5 cm

Ⓑ 6.0 cm

Ⓒ 6.5 cm

Ⓓ 7.0 cm

The graph below shows how many students in each grade ride their bikes to Newton School each day. Use the graph to answer questions 36–38.

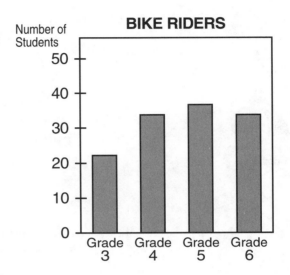

36. In which grade do the greatest number of students ride their bikes to school?

Ⓐ Grade 3   Ⓒ Grade 5

Ⓑ Grade 4   Ⓓ Grade 6

37. How many third graders ride their bikes to school?

Ⓐ 20   Ⓒ 25

Ⓑ 23   Ⓓ 35

38. How many more students in Grade 5 ride their bikes to school than in Grade 6?

Ⓐ 3   Ⓒ 12

Ⓑ 5   Ⓓ 38

Number Correct/Total = _____ /38

Whole Number Concepts

Recognizing, comparing, and ordering numerals

Hey, I'm fifteen not fifty-one!

Directions: Choose the best answer for each question.

A Which numeral means the same as fifty-one?

   Ⓐ 15   Ⓒ 150

   Ⓑ 51   Ⓓ 510

B Which is another name for 6 hundreds, 2 tens, and 5 ones?

   Ⓐ 6025   Ⓒ 625

   Ⓑ 652   Ⓓ 6205

These questions are about **renaming numbers**. In Example A, the question asks you to rename the number word *fifty-one* as a numeral. To answer this question, say the number word to yourself and think about what it means. The number *fifty-one* has 5 tens and 1 one. Answer Ⓑ, *51*, has 5 tens and 1 one. Choice Ⓑ is the correct answer. The other choices stand for the numbers *fifteen*, choice Ⓐ, *one hundred fifty*, choice Ⓒ, and *five hundred ten*, choice Ⓓ.

Example B asks you to rename 6 hundreds, 2 tens, and 5 ones as a numeral. To answer this question, you can use your scratch paper to write the numbers in a chart like this.

Thousands	Hundreds	Tens	Ones
	6	2	5

Or, you can look at the answer choices and find a numeral with a 6 in the hundreds place. Then find the numeral that has a 2 in the tens place and a 5 in the ones place. The answer is Ⓒ, *625*. Watch out for answer choices such as Ⓑ, *652*. It has the same numbers but in different order.

Now let's look at some more test question examples on page 107.

C Which number is between 533 and 687?

Ⓐ 521

Ⓑ 472

Ⓒ 693

Ⓓ 590

D What number is 10 more than 230?

Ⓐ 240

Ⓑ 1230

Ⓒ 231

Ⓓ 330

These questions ask you to **compare numbers** and put them in order. Example C asks you to find the number that is between 533 and 687. This means that the number must be more than 533 and less than 687. Choices Ⓐ and Ⓑ are less than 533, so they are not correct. Choice Ⓒ is more than 687, so it is not correct. Choice Ⓓ, *590*, is more than 533 and less than 687, so it is the correct answer.

Example D asks you for the number that is 10 more than 230. To answer this question, add 10 in the tens place. 230 plus 10 is 240. Choice Ⓐ is correct.

Now look at these examples.

E Which numeral has a 6 in the hundreds place?

Ⓐ 6512   Ⓒ 1562

Ⓑ 5612   Ⓓ 2156

F What is the value of the 3 in 4234?

Ⓐ 3000   Ⓒ 30

Ⓑ 300   Ⓓ 3

These questions are about **place value**, or the value of each number. To answer these questions, you can write the numbers on your scratch paper in a chart (as you saw in Example B). Or, you can say the number in words as you saw in Example B.

In Example E, the only number that has a 6 in the hundreds place is choice Ⓑ, *5612*. In words, this number is "five thousand *six hundred* twelve."

In Example F, the number is four thousand two hundred *thirty*-four. The 3 is in the tens place. It has the value of 3 tens, or 30. Choice Ⓒ is correct.

Test-Taking Tips

1 Look for key words in each question. (In Example C, the key word is *between*. In Example D, the key words are *more than*.)

2 Try out each answer choice until you find the one that is correct.

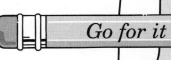

Go for it

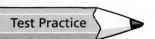

Test Practice 1: Whole Number Concepts   Time: **20** minutes

Directions: Choose the best answer for each question.

1. Which numeral means three hundred two?

   Ⓐ 302
   Ⓑ 320
   Ⓒ 3002
   Ⓓ 3020

2. Which numeral stands for one thousand thirty-four?

   Ⓐ 10034
   Ⓑ   134
   Ⓒ   1034
   Ⓓ   1304

3. Which is another name for nine?

   Ⓐ 10 + 1
   Ⓑ   8 + 1
   Ⓒ   3 + 3
   Ⓓ   4 × 5

4. What is another name for 85?

   Ⓐ 6 tens and 15 ones
   Ⓑ 7 tens and 5 ones
   Ⓒ 8 tens and 15 ones
   Ⓓ 7 tens and 15 ones

5. What is another name for 6 thousands, 3 hundreds, and 1 ten?

   Ⓐ 6031
   Ⓑ 6310
   Ⓒ 6301
   Ⓓ   631

6. Which is another name for 7020?

   Ⓐ 7 + 20
   Ⓑ 70 + 20
   Ⓒ 7000 + 200
   Ⓓ 7000 + 20

7. Which number stands for

   | 400 + 40 + 1 | ?

   Ⓐ   4041
   Ⓑ   441
   Ⓒ   414
   Ⓓ 40410

8. Which number is one more than 839?

   Ⓐ 838
   Ⓑ 840
   Ⓒ 841
   Ⓓ 849

GO ON

9. What number is one less than 31?

   Ⓐ 21   Ⓒ 30
   Ⓑ 29   Ⓓ 32

10. Which number makes this sentence true?

    90 > ▢

    Ⓐ 100   Ⓒ 90
    Ⓑ 91   Ⓓ 89

11. What number does this chart show?

Hundreds	Tens	Ones
|||	⊬⊬|	||

    Ⓐ 532   Ⓒ 352
    Ⓑ 524   Ⓓ 325

12. Each bundle has 10 caps. How many caps are there in all?

    Ⓐ 7   Ⓒ 34
    Ⓑ 32   Ⓓ 43

13. Which elephant is second in line?

    Ⓐ   Ⓑ   Ⓒ   Ⓓ

14. If there are 6 people in front of you in line, which place in line do you have?

    Ⓐ 5th
    Ⓑ 6th
    Ⓒ 7th
    Ⓓ 8th

15. Which number is between 420 and 425?

    Ⓐ 429
    Ⓑ 410
    Ⓒ 430
    Ⓓ 423

16. Which group of numbers is in order from greatest to least?

    Ⓐ 633, 391, 562
    Ⓑ 391, 562, 633
    Ⓒ 562, 633, 391
    Ⓓ 633, 562, 391

GO ON

17. What does the 7 stand for in 4174?

    Ⓐ 7 tens
    Ⓑ 7 ones
    Ⓒ 7 hundreds
    Ⓓ 7 thousands

18. Which numeral has 9 hundreds and 5 ones?

    Ⓐ 95
    Ⓑ 905
    Ⓒ 950
    Ⓓ 509

19. Look at the number pattern below. Which number fits in the blank?

    8, 18, 28, ___

    Ⓐ 29
    Ⓑ 38
    Ⓒ 48
    Ⓓ 108

20. What number is missing from the pattern below?

    3, 6, 9, ___, 15

    Ⓐ 18
    Ⓑ 14
    Ⓒ 13
    Ⓓ 12

21. What is 1234 rounded to the nearest hundred?

    Ⓐ 1000
    Ⓑ 1230
    Ⓒ 1300
    Ⓓ 1200

22. Which pair of numbers has only even numbers?

    Ⓐ 11, 12
    Ⓑ 10, 15
    Ⓒ 4, 16
    Ⓓ 1, 30

23. Which number is about equal to

    31 + 58 ?

    Ⓐ 90
    Ⓑ 80
    Ⓒ 100
    Ⓓ 95

24. Which number is closest to

    103 − 69 ?

    Ⓐ 70
    Ⓑ 50
    Ⓒ 40
    Ⓓ 30

STOP

Number Correct/Total = _____ /24

Fractions and Decimals

Comparing and renaming fractions and decimals

Does Mom know you're going to eat 1/4 of that pie?

Directions: Choose the best answer for each question.

A Which fraction has the greatest value?

ⓐ $\frac{1}{4}$ ⓒ $\frac{1}{3}$

ⓑ $\frac{1}{2}$ ⓓ $\frac{1}{6}$

B Which is less than 0.02?

ⓐ 0.20   ⓒ 0.002

ⓑ 2.00   ⓓ 0.10

To answer Example A, you must rename each fraction so it has the same **denominator** (the number on the bottom). Then you can compare like fractions.

$$\frac{1}{4} = \frac{3}{12} \qquad \frac{1}{2} = \frac{6}{12} \qquad \frac{1}{3} = \frac{4}{12} \qquad \frac{1}{6} = \frac{2}{12}$$

If you compare these fractions, you can see that the one with the greatest value is $\frac{6}{12}$. This is the same as $\frac{1}{2}$, so choice ⓑ is correct.

Example B asks you to find the decimal that is less than 0.02. Each number in the decimal has a place value. Use the chart below to see the place value of each number.

Ones	Tenths	Hundredths	Thousandths
2.00 = 2	0.2 = $\frac{2}{10}$	0.02 = $\frac{2}{100}$	0.002 = $\frac{2}{1000}$

The decimal 0.02 means $\frac{2}{100}$. Choice ⓒ, *0.002*, is less than $\frac{2}{100}$. It means the same as $\frac{2}{1000}$. Choice ⓒ is correct.

Test-Taking Tips

1 Look for key words in each question. (In Example A, the key word is *greatest*. In Example B, the key words are *less than*.)

2 When comparing fractions, rename them as like fractions (with the same denominator), as in $\frac{1}{2} = \frac{6}{12}$.

3 When comparing decimals, find the place value of each number.

Go for it

Test Practice 2: Fractions and Decimals   Time: **10** minutes

Directions: Choose the best answer for each question.

1. Which shape has $\frac{2}{3}$ shaded?

   Ⓐ   Ⓒ

   Ⓑ   Ⓓ

2. What fraction of the figure is shaded?

   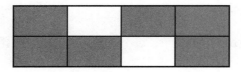

   Ⓐ $\frac{1}{3}$ Ⓒ $\frac{2}{3}$

   Ⓑ $\frac{3}{4}$ Ⓓ $\frac{3}{2}$

3. Which fraction is greater than $\frac{3}{5}$?

   Ⓐ $\frac{2}{4}$ Ⓒ $\frac{2}{5}$

   Ⓑ $\frac{1}{3}$ Ⓓ $\frac{7}{10}$

4. Which fraction has the greatest value?

   Ⓐ $\frac{1}{2}$ Ⓒ $\frac{2}{3}$

   Ⓑ $\frac{4}{6}$ Ⓓ $\frac{6}{8}$

5. Which fraction is another name for $\frac{5}{6}$?

   Ⓐ $\frac{11}{12}$ Ⓒ $\frac{15}{18}$

   Ⓑ $\frac{2}{3}$ Ⓓ $\frac{18}{24}$

6. What is another name for $\frac{12}{20}$?

   Ⓐ $\frac{3}{4}$ Ⓒ $\frac{6}{8}$

   Ⓑ $\frac{5}{10}$ Ⓓ $\frac{3}{5}$

7. Which decimal has the least value?

   Ⓐ 1.50   Ⓒ .015

   Ⓑ .150   Ⓓ 15.0

8. Which decimal is greater than 0.330?

   Ⓐ 3.300   Ⓒ 0.033

   Ⓑ 0.303   Ⓓ 0.003

9. Which decimal is between 0.45 and 0.64?

   Ⓐ 5.50   Ⓒ 0.054

   Ⓑ 0.53   Ⓓ 0.350

10. Which group of decimals is in order from greatest to least?

    Ⓐ 6.672, 6.762, 6.627

    Ⓑ 6.762, 6.672, 6.627

    Ⓒ 6.627, 6.672, 6.762

    Ⓓ 6.672, 6.627, 6.762

Number Correct/Total = _____ /10

112

MATH
Lesson 3

Using Numbers
Solving number sentences

A Which number sentence goes with the picture below?

Ⓐ 3 + 1 = 4   Ⓒ 4 − 1 = 3

Ⓑ 3 − 1 = 2   Ⓓ 2 + 2 = 4

B Which number best completes the number sentence below?

4 + 2 = 6

6 = ☐ + 4

Ⓐ 4   Ⓒ 10

Ⓑ 6   Ⓓ 2

These questions are about **number sentences** and **properties of numbers**. Example A asks you to find a number sentence that matches the picture. The picture shows 4 birds. One of the birds is flying away, and 3 are left on the fence. The number sentence should be 4 birds − 1 bird = 3 birds. Choice Ⓒ is correct.

You can answer Example B if you know that when you add numbers, the order of the numbers does not matter. The answer is still the same no matter which number is listed first in the number sentence. Example B gives two number sentences.
If 4 + 2 = 6, then 2 + 4 must also be 6. The number that completes the number sentence is 2. Choice Ⓓ is correct.

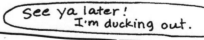

See ya later!
I'm ducking out.

Hint

You can practice at home by using numbers and number sentences to figure out the answers to common problems. For example, you may want to find how many socks you have left if you take two out. To do this you can write a number sentence and use it to solve your problem.

Test-Taking Tips

1 Read each number sentence and look at any pictures carefully.

2 Try out each answer choice until you find one that is correct.

Go for it

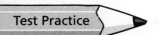

Test Practice 3: Using Numbers

Time: **8** minutes

Directions: Choose the best answer for each question.

1. Milt bought a 40-pound bag of food for his dog. After two weeks, there were 33 pounds left. Which number sentence could you use to find how much his dog ate in two weeks?

   Ⓐ $40 - 33 = \square$

   Ⓑ $33 - \square = 40$

   Ⓒ $40 \div 33 = \square$

   Ⓓ $33 + 40 = \square$

2. Which number sentence goes with the picture below?

   Ⓐ $3 - 1 = 2$

   Ⓑ $3 \times 1 = 3$

   Ⓒ $3 + 1 = 4$

   Ⓓ $4 - 1 = 3$

3. Lisa cracked 8 eggs into 2 bowls. Which number sentence shows how to find how many she put in each bowl if she put the same number in each bowl?

   Ⓐ $8 - 2 = \square$

   Ⓑ $2 + 8 = \square$

   Ⓒ $2 \times 8 = \square$

   Ⓓ $8 \div 2 = \square$

4. Which number sentence goes with the picture below?

   Ⓐ $3 \times 4 = 12$

   Ⓑ $3 + 4 = 7$

   Ⓒ $4 - 3 = 1$

   Ⓓ $12 - 3 = 4$

5. Which number makes this number sentence true?

   $$14 - 2 = 13 - \square$$

   Ⓐ 1   Ⓒ 3

   Ⓑ 2   Ⓓ 4

6. If $22 + n = 44$, what is the value of n?

   Ⓐ 2   Ⓒ 20

   Ⓑ 12   Ⓓ 22

7. Which number best completes this number sentence?

   $$15 - 3 = \square$$

   Ⓐ 4   Ⓒ 12

   Ⓑ 5   Ⓓ 18

GO ON

8. Solve to find n.

$$4 \times 8 = n$$

Ⓐ 4   Ⓒ 32

Ⓑ 16   Ⓓ 48

9. Which sign goes in the circle?

$$10 \bigcirc 2 = 5 \times 4$$

Ⓐ +   Ⓒ ×

Ⓑ −   Ⓓ ÷

10. Which sign goes in the circle?

$$2 + 7 = 18 \bigcirc 9$$

Ⓐ ×   Ⓒ ÷

Ⓑ +   Ⓓ −

11. Which sign goes in the circle?

$$35 \bigcirc 5 = 7$$

Ⓐ ÷   Ⓒ +

Ⓑ ×   Ⓓ −

12. Which is another way to write

$$2 \times 4 \ ?$$

Ⓐ 4 + 2

Ⓑ 2 × 2 × 2 × 2

Ⓒ 4 − 2

Ⓓ 2 + 2 + 2 + 2

13. Which number sentence goes with

$$6 + 7 = 13 \ ?$$

Ⓐ 13 − 6 = 7

Ⓑ 6 × 7 = 42

Ⓒ 7 − 6 = 1

Ⓓ 13 + 7 = 20

14. Which number fits in the boxes to make both of these number sentences true?

$$15 \times \square = \square \times 15$$

$$\square \times 15 = 15$$

Ⓐ 0   Ⓒ 5

Ⓑ 1   Ⓓ 15

15. Which number makes this number sentence true?

$$\square + 10 = 10$$

Ⓐ 0   Ⓒ 5

Ⓑ 1   Ⓓ 10

16. What number completes this number sentence?

$$(4 + 7) + 1 = 4 + (\square + 1)$$

Ⓐ 1   Ⓒ 7

Ⓑ 4   Ⓓ 12

Number Correct/Total = _____ /16

115

Addition and Subtraction

Adding and subtracting whole numbers

87 spots

Directions: Choose the best answer for each question. If the correct answer is not given, choose NG.

A   87
    + 293

Ⓐ 280
Ⓑ 370
Ⓒ 380
Ⓓ 390
Ⓔ NG

B   455
    − 42

Ⓐ 497
Ⓑ 423
Ⓒ 403
Ⓓ 313
Ⓔ NG

Look at Example A. When you add numbers with more than one digit, use what you learned about place value. Remember to carry the 1 in each column (as shown in the picture). 87 + 293 = 380. Choice Ⓒ is correct.

You can check your addition by adding the numbers in different order.

$$87 + 293 = 380 \qquad 293 + 87 = 380$$

To solve the problem in Example B, you have to subtract: 455 − 42 = 413. This is the answer to the problem, 413. But 413 is not one of the answer choices. The correct answer is "Not Given." The directions say that "If the correct answer is not given, choose NG." NG stands for "Not Given," so you should mark choice Ⓔ, *NG*.

87
+293

293 spots

Test-Taking Tips

1 Look at the sign first to see if you should add (+) or subtract (−).

2 Check the answer to a subtraction problem by adding. (In Example B, 413 + 42 = 455, so you know that 413 is correct.)

Go for it

Test Practice 4: Addition and Subtraction   Time: **20** minutes

Directions: Choose the best answer for each question.

1.
$$\begin{array}{r} 66 \\ 44 \\ +\ 22 \\ \hline \end{array}$$
- Ⓐ 122
- Ⓑ 130
- Ⓒ 132
- Ⓓ 134
- Ⓔ NG

2.
$$\begin{array}{r} 17 \\ +\ 71 \\ \hline \end{array}$$
- Ⓐ 66
- Ⓑ 78
- Ⓒ 86
- Ⓓ 88
- Ⓔ NG

3.
$$\begin{array}{r} 43 \\ -\ 11 \\ \hline \end{array}$$
- Ⓐ 22
- Ⓑ 32
- Ⓒ 34
- Ⓓ 42
- Ⓔ NG

4.
$$\begin{array}{r} 114 \\ -\ 63 \\ \hline \end{array}$$
- Ⓐ 57
- Ⓑ 51
- Ⓒ 47
- Ⓓ 41
- Ⓔ NG

5.
$$\begin{array}{r} 91 \\ -\ 8 \\ \hline \end{array}$$
- Ⓐ 84
- Ⓑ 82
- Ⓒ 73
- Ⓓ 11
- Ⓔ NG

6.
$$\begin{array}{r} 415 \\ +\ 27 \\ \hline \end{array}$$
- Ⓐ 622
- Ⓑ 488
- Ⓒ 442
- Ⓓ 432
- Ⓔ NG

7.
$$\begin{array}{r} 793 \\ -\ 587 \\ \hline \end{array}$$
- Ⓐ 206
- Ⓑ 207
- Ⓒ 216
- Ⓓ 306
- Ⓔ NG

8.
$$\begin{array}{r} 89 \\ +\ 9 \\ \hline \end{array}$$
- Ⓐ 78
- Ⓑ 80
- Ⓒ 88
- Ⓓ 98
- Ⓔ NG

9.
$$\begin{array}{r} 533 \\ 21 \\ +\ 5 \\ \hline \end{array}$$
- Ⓐ 748
- Ⓑ 568
- Ⓒ 569
- Ⓓ 558
- Ⓔ NG

10.
$$\begin{array}{r} 76 \\ -\ 67 \\ \hline \end{array}$$
- Ⓐ 9
- Ⓑ 10
- Ⓒ 13
- Ⓓ 19
- Ⓔ NG

11.
$$\begin{array}{r} 679 \\ +\ 7 \\ \hline \end{array}$$
- Ⓐ 749
- Ⓑ 686
- Ⓒ 676
- Ⓓ 649
- Ⓔ NG

12.
$$\begin{array}{r} 52 \\ -\ 28 \\ \hline \end{array}$$
- Ⓐ 36
- Ⓑ 34
- Ⓒ 26
- Ⓓ 24
- Ⓔ NG

GO ON

13.   37 − 19 =

Ⓐ 16
Ⓑ 18
Ⓒ 28
Ⓓ 32
Ⓔ NG

14.   305
        28
      + 295

Ⓐ 528
Ⓑ 618
Ⓒ 623
Ⓓ 628
Ⓔ NG

15.   47 + 62 =

Ⓐ 99
Ⓑ 105
Ⓒ 109
Ⓓ 110
Ⓔ NG

16.   681
      − 90

Ⓐ 511
Ⓑ 591
Ⓒ 671
Ⓓ 691
Ⓔ NG

17.   100
      − 45

Ⓐ 35
Ⓑ 45
Ⓒ 55
Ⓓ 65
Ⓔ NG

18.   76 − 33 =

Ⓐ 33
Ⓑ 43
Ⓒ 49
Ⓓ 109
Ⓔ NG

19.   898
        50
      + 42

Ⓐ 990
Ⓑ 986
Ⓒ 980
Ⓓ 880
Ⓔ NG

20.   78 + 44 =

Ⓐ 109
Ⓑ 117
Ⓒ 118
Ⓓ 120
Ⓔ NG

21.   21
       463
     + 556

Ⓐ 940
Ⓑ 941
Ⓒ 1039
Ⓓ 1040
Ⓔ NG

22.   310
      − 155

Ⓐ 155
Ⓑ 165
Ⓒ 255
Ⓓ 275
Ⓔ NG

23.   84 − 65 =

Ⓐ 18
Ⓑ 19
Ⓒ 22
Ⓓ 28
Ⓔ NG

24.   656
      + 17

Ⓐ 773
Ⓑ 763
Ⓒ 674
Ⓓ 673
Ⓔ NG

Number Correct/Total = _____ /24

Multiplication and Division

Multiplying and dividing whole numbers

OLLIE the Outrageous Octopus

Directions: Choose the best answer for each question.

A   17
      × 8

   Ⓐ 25
   Ⓑ 87
   Ⓒ 128
   Ⓓ 136
   Ⓔ NG

B 4)48

   Ⓐ 10
   Ⓑ 11
   Ⓒ 12
   Ⓓ 14
   Ⓔ NG

To solve Example A, you must multiply. On your scratch paper, first multiply 8×7 to get 56. Put the 6 in the ones column of your answer and carry the 5 to the tens column. Write it above the 1 in 17 so that you will not forget it when you do the next step. Now multiply 8×1 to get 8, and add the 5 that you carried to get 13. Write the 13 next to the 6 in your answer. $17 \times 8 = 136$. Choice Ⓓ, *136*, is correct.

To solve Example B, you must divide. 48 divided by 4 equals 12. The correct answer is choice Ⓒ. Remember: If the correct answer is not given, choose NG.

Test-Taking Tips

1 Look at the sign to see if you should multiply or divide. The "multiply" sign may be an × or a dot: 17×8 or $17 \cdot 8$.

The "divide" sign may be a), a ÷, or a line: 4)48 or $48 \div 4$ or $48/4$.

2 Check the answers to division problems by multiplying. (In Example B, $4 \times 12 = 48$, so 12 is the correct answer.)

Go for it

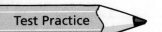

Test Practice 5: Multiplication and Division   Time: 20 minutes

Directions: Choose the best answer for each question.

1.
$$6 \times 3$$
- Ⓐ 9
- Ⓑ 12
- Ⓒ 18
- Ⓓ 24
- Ⓔ NG

6.
$$61 \times 8$$
- Ⓐ 148
- Ⓑ 448
- Ⓒ 468
- Ⓓ 488
- Ⓔ NG

2. $7 \times 7 =$
- Ⓐ 49
- Ⓑ 48
- Ⓒ 35
- Ⓓ 14
- Ⓔ NG

7.
$$89 \times 9$$
- Ⓐ 801
- Ⓑ 810
- Ⓒ 818
- Ⓓ 901
- Ⓔ NG

3. $8 \times 4 =$
- Ⓐ 30
- Ⓑ 32
- Ⓒ 34
- Ⓓ 36
- Ⓔ NG

8.
$$743 \times 2$$
- Ⓐ 965
- Ⓑ 1485
- Ⓒ 1486
- Ⓓ 1580
- Ⓔ NG

4.
$$13 \times 2$$
- Ⓐ 15
- Ⓑ 23
- Ⓒ 25
- Ⓓ 26
- Ⓔ NG

9.
$$471 \times 3$$
- Ⓐ 1203
- Ⓑ 1223
- Ⓒ 1403
- Ⓓ 1413
- Ⓔ NG

5.
$$33 \times 5$$
- Ⓐ 85
- Ⓑ 95
- Ⓒ 155
- Ⓓ 165
- Ⓔ NG

10. $113 \times 5 =$
- Ⓐ 555
- Ⓑ 565
- Ⓒ 653
- Ⓓ 665
- Ⓔ NG

GO ON

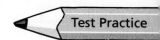
11. 38 × 11 =

Ⓐ 318
Ⓑ 328
Ⓒ 408
Ⓓ 418
Ⓔ NG

12. 6)‾36‾

Ⓐ 3
Ⓑ 5
Ⓒ 6
Ⓓ 8
Ⓔ NG

13. 12 ÷ 3 =

Ⓐ 8
Ⓑ 6
Ⓒ 4
Ⓓ 3
Ⓔ NG

14. 9)‾63‾

Ⓐ 7
Ⓑ 8
Ⓒ 9
Ⓓ 10
Ⓔ NG

15. 5)‾25‾

Ⓐ 3
Ⓑ 4
Ⓒ 5
Ⓓ 7
Ⓔ NG

16. 121 ÷ 11 =

Ⓐ 10
Ⓑ 11
Ⓒ 12
Ⓓ 13
Ⓔ NG

17. 4)‾64‾

Ⓐ 12
Ⓑ 16
Ⓒ 18
Ⓓ 20
Ⓔ NG

18. 96 ÷ 6 =

Ⓐ 11
Ⓑ 13
Ⓒ 16
Ⓓ 26
Ⓔ NG

19. 2)‾78‾

Ⓐ 34
Ⓑ 36
Ⓒ 41
Ⓓ 44
Ⓔ NG

20. 39 ÷ 3 =

Ⓐ 9
Ⓑ 11
Ⓒ 12
Ⓓ 13
Ⓔ NG

21. 98 ÷ 7 =

Ⓐ 14
Ⓑ 13
Ⓒ 9
Ⓓ 8
Ⓔ NG

22. 3)‾75‾

Ⓐ 23
Ⓑ 24
Ⓒ 25
Ⓓ 30
Ⓔ NG

Number Correct/Total = _____ /22

Working with Fractions and Decimals

Adding and subtracting fractions and decimals

Directions: Choose the best answer for each question.

A $\frac{1}{5} + \frac{2}{5} =$

    Ⓐ $\frac{3}{10}$

    Ⓑ $\frac{4}{5}$

    Ⓒ $\frac{3}{5}$

    Ⓓ $\frac{1}{5}$

    Ⓔ NG

B $\begin{array}{r} \$42.30 \\ -\ 21.05 \\ \hline \end{array}$

    Ⓐ $21.25

    Ⓑ $21.35

    Ⓒ $20.25

    Ⓓ $20.20

    Ⓔ NG

42.30 −21.05 = ?

In a fraction, the number on the top is called the **numerator**. The number on the bottom is the **denominator**. In Example A, both fractions have the denominator 5. To add fractions with the same denominator, add their numerators and keep the denominators the same. In Example A, then, you add $1 + 2$ to get 3. The correct answer to the problem $\frac{1}{5} + \frac{2}{5}$ is $\frac{3}{5}$, choice Ⓒ.

To answer Example B, you have to subtract money amounts, which are written as decimals. To subtract decimals, line up the numbers so that the decimal points are right under each other. Then subtract as you would with whole numbers. The correct answer is choice Ⓐ, *$21.25*. Remember: If the correct answer is not given, mark NG.

Test-Taking Tips

1 When fractions have the same denominator, add or subtract only the numerators.

2 Remember to always reduce fractions to their smallest parts. (Example:

$\frac{5}{10} = \frac{1}{2}$; $\frac{3}{9} = \frac{1}{3}$; $\frac{4}{6} = \frac{2}{3}$, etc.)

When looking for the correct answer to a problem with fractions, look for the one that has been reduced.

3 Check the answers to subtraction problems by adding. (In Example B, $21.25 + $21.05 = $42.30.)

Go for it

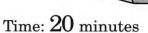

Test Practice 6:
Working with Fractions and Decimals

Time: **20** minutes

Directions: Choose the best answer for each question.

1. $\frac{7}{9} - \frac{5}{9} =$ Ⓐ $\frac{2}{9}$ Ⓓ $\frac{12}{18}$

    Ⓑ $\frac{5}{9}$ Ⓔ NG

    Ⓒ $\frac{4}{9}$

6. $4\frac{5}{7} - \frac{3}{7} =$ Ⓐ $4\frac{2}{7}$ Ⓓ $3\frac{2}{7}$

    Ⓑ $4\frac{2}{14}$ Ⓔ NG

    Ⓒ $3\frac{1}{7}$

2. $1\frac{3}{5} + 2\frac{2}{5} =$ Ⓐ 3   Ⓓ 4

    Ⓑ $3\frac{1}{5}$ Ⓔ NG

    Ⓒ $3\frac{4}{5}$

7. $\frac{11}{20} - \frac{3}{20} =$ Ⓐ $\frac{9}{10}$ Ⓓ $\frac{9}{20}$

    Ⓑ $\frac{2}{5}$ Ⓔ NG

    Ⓒ $\frac{3}{4}$

3. $\frac{1}{8} + \frac{3}{8} =$ Ⓐ $\frac{1}{2}$ Ⓓ $\frac{5}{8}$

    Ⓑ 1   Ⓔ NG

    Ⓒ $\frac{1}{4}$

8. $10\frac{8}{10}$ Ⓐ $\frac{1}{10}$ Ⓓ $2\frac{5}{10}$

   $-\ 9\frac{7}{10}$ Ⓑ $\frac{1}{5}$ Ⓔ NG

    Ⓒ $1\frac{1}{10}$

4. $3\frac{2}{3}$ Ⓐ $2\frac{2}{3}$ Ⓓ 1

   $-1\frac{1}{3}$ Ⓑ 2   Ⓔ NG

    Ⓒ $1\frac{1}{3}$

9. $\frac{4}{5} + \frac{3}{5} =$ Ⓐ $\frac{1}{5}$ Ⓓ $1\frac{2}{5}$

    Ⓑ $\frac{7}{10}$ Ⓔ NG

    Ⓒ $1\frac{1}{5}$

5. $\frac{5}{16} + \frac{2}{16} =$ Ⓐ $\frac{7}{8}$ Ⓓ $\frac{3}{8}$

    Ⓑ $\frac{7}{16}$ Ⓔ NG

    Ⓒ $\frac{2}{4}$

10. $6\frac{3}{4}$ Ⓐ $2\frac{1}{4}$ Ⓓ $4\frac{1}{2}$

    $-2\frac{2}{4}$ Ⓑ $3\frac{1}{2}$ Ⓔ NG

    Ⓒ 4

GO ON

11.　1.21 − 0.11 =

Ⓐ 0.10
Ⓑ 1.09
Ⓒ 1.10
Ⓓ 1.11
Ⓔ NG

16.　$19.99
　　− 11.29

Ⓐ $10.79
Ⓑ $ 9.79
Ⓒ $ 9.70
Ⓓ $ 8.79
Ⓔ NG

12.　$5.99
　　− 1.49

Ⓐ $4.40
Ⓑ $4.50
Ⓒ $4.59
Ⓓ $6.50
Ⓔ NG

17.　7.18 + 0.34 =

Ⓐ 7.54
Ⓑ 7.52
Ⓒ 7.44
Ⓓ 6.52
Ⓔ NG

13.　18.07
　　+ 5.06

Ⓐ 13.13
Ⓑ 23.01
Ⓒ 23.13
Ⓓ 24.01
Ⓔ NG

18.　$15.35
　　+ 29.62

Ⓐ $43.97
Ⓑ $44.87
Ⓒ $44.93
Ⓓ $44.97
Ⓔ NG

14.　$48.88
　　− 22.14

Ⓐ $26.74
Ⓑ $26.94
Ⓒ $46.64
Ⓓ $66.74
Ⓔ NG

19.　30.33
　　− 5.25

Ⓐ 24.08
Ⓑ 24.18
Ⓒ 25.02
Ⓓ 25.08
Ⓔ NG

15.　33.01
　　+ 31.30

Ⓐ 63.04
Ⓑ 63.31
Ⓒ 64.04
Ⓓ 64.31
Ⓔ NG

20.　$0.69
　　+ $0.69

Ⓐ $1.28
Ⓑ $1.29
Ⓒ $1.38
Ⓓ $1.39
Ⓔ NG

Number Correct/Total = _____ /20

Problem Solving

Solving word problems

Directions: Choose the best answer for each question.

A Susanna spent $.89 on a card. She gave the clerk $5.00. Which number sentence should you use to find how much change Susanna should get?

Ⓐ $5.00 × $.89 = ☐

Ⓑ $5.00 + ☐ = $.89

Ⓒ $5.00 − $.89 = ☐

Ⓓ ☐ − $.89 = $5.00

Ⓔ NG

B Marv made $18 selling lemonade at the fair. What other information do you need to find out how many cups of lemonade Marv sold?

Ⓐ how long Marv worked

Ⓑ how much lemonade was in each cup

Ⓒ how many people were at the fair

Ⓓ how many people bought two cups

Ⓔ how much each cup cost

Example A asks you to find the number sentence that will help you solve the problem. To answer Example A, read over the information given in the problem and make sure you know what you are trying to figure out (how much change Susanna should get). Then write a number sentence. To find out how much change Susanna should get back after she spends $.89 of her $5.00, you should subtract $.89 from $5.00. The number sentence would be written as $5.00 − $.89 = ☐. Choice Ⓒ is correct.

Example B asks you to identify information that you need to know to solve a problem. You already know how much total money Marv made. To find out how many cups of lemonade he sold, you also need to know how much each cup cost. The amount Marv made ($18) divided by the amount each cup cost would give you the number of cups he sold. Choice Ⓔ is correct.

Now look at some more test question examples on page 126.

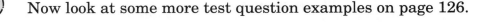

C Marge has filled 13 pages in her picture album. The album has 26 total pages. How many pages does Marge have left to fill?

- Ⓐ 39
- Ⓑ 23
- Ⓒ 13
- Ⓓ 2
- Ⓔ NG

D Julio worked on his model plane 2 hours a day for 3 days. He worked on it for 3 more hours the next day. How many total hours did Julio spend on his model?

- Ⓐ 3
- Ⓑ 6
- Ⓒ 8
- Ⓓ 9
- Ⓔ NG

To answer Example C, you must subtract. If Marge's album has 26 pages in all, and she has used 13 of them, then you should subtract to find out how many pages are left. Set up the problem like this:

26 total pages − 13 pages used = ☐ pages left.
Since 26 − 13 = 13, the correct answer is choice Ⓒ.

Example D is a word problem with two steps. Follow these steps to find the answer.

1) How many hours did Julio work in the first 3 days?
   3 days × 2 hours a day = 6 hours
2) How many hours did Julio work in all?
   6 hours + 3 hours = 9 hours

The correct answer is choice Ⓓ, *9 hours*, because Julio worked 6 hours in the first 3 days and 3 hours the next day.

Test-Taking Tips

1 Look for key words and numbers to help you solve each problem. (In Example A, the key words are *how much change*. The key numbers are *$.89* and *$5.00*.)

2 Make sure you know what to look for in each problem. Then write a number sentence to help you solve it. (In Example C, you are looking for the number of pages left in the album. The number sentence would be 26 − 13 = ☐.)

Go for it

Test Practice 7 : Problem Solving

Time: **15** minutes

Directions: Choose the best answer for each question.

1. Ron caught 30 fish in 5 days. Which number sentence should you use to find how many fish he caught each day?

   ⓐ 30 ÷ 5 = ☐

   ⓑ 30 × 5 = ☐

   ⓒ 30 + 5 = ☐

   ⓓ 30 − 5 = ☐

   ⓔ NG

2. Lee had 4 bags of 12 mints each. She ate 3 mints. Which operation must you use to solve the second step of this problem if you want to find out how many mints Lee has left?

   ⓐ 48 ÷ 3 = ☐

   ⓑ 48 × 3 = ☐

   ⓒ 48 + 3 = ☐

   ⓓ 48 − 3 = ☐

   ⓔ NG

3. Cal picked 5 pounds of beans and 2 pounds of peas. Which number sentence will help you find out how many pounds of vegetables Cal picked in all?

   ⓐ 5 × 2 = ☐

   ⓑ 5 − ☐ = 2

   ⓒ 2 + ☐ = 5

   ⓓ 5 + 2 = ☐

   ⓔ NG

4. Three stamps cost $.45. How much does one stamp cost?

   ⓐ $ .12   ⓒ $1.35   ⓔ NG

   ⓑ $ .15   ⓓ $1.50

5. Kari checked 9 books out of the library. So far she has read 6 of them. How many does she have left to read?

   ⓐ 15   ⓒ 4   ⓔ NG

   ⓑ 5   ⓓ 3

6. Mark's Math class ends at 1:55. His next class begins at 2:05. How many minutes does he have between classes?

   ⓐ 5   ⓒ 30   ⓔ NG

   ⓑ 10   ⓓ 50

7. Nick and Liz made 15 paper flowers for the school play. The next day they made twice as many as they did the first day. How many flowers did they make in all?

   ⓐ 17   ⓒ 32   ⓔ NG

   ⓑ 30   ⓓ 45

8. At school Al sits in front of Sam. Sam sits in front of Beth. Beth sits between Al and Sam. Wendy sits behind Sam. Todd sits in front of Al. Who sits closest to the front ?

   ⓐ Al   ⓒ Beth   ⓔ Todd

   ⓑ Sam   ⓓ Wendy

GO ON

9. Kim got $10 for her birthday. She spent $4.50 on a book. Then she spent $3.00 on a movie ticket. How much money does she have left?

Ⓐ $2.00   Ⓓ $7.50
Ⓑ $5.00   Ⓔ NG
Ⓒ $7.00

10. Last fall Ed was 48 inches tall. Now he is 54 inches tall. How many inches has Ed grown?

Ⓐ 4   Ⓒ 8   Ⓔ NG
Ⓑ 6   Ⓓ 16

11. There are 36 desks in a classroom. The desks are in 4 rows with the same number of desks in each row. How many desks are in each row?

Ⓐ 6   Ⓒ 9   Ⓔ NG
Ⓑ 8   Ⓓ 32

12. Lil bought 4 packs of baseball cards. Each pack had 10 cards. She traded 7 of her new cards for a baseball. How many cards did Lil have left?

Ⓐ 40   Ⓒ 17   Ⓔ NG
Ⓑ 33   Ⓓ 3

13. Jo's piano lesson is at 3:30. She plays for 45 minutes. What time does she finish?

Ⓐ 4:00   Ⓒ 4:20   Ⓔ NG
Ⓑ 4:15   Ⓓ 4:45

14. Jake hung 4 clean shirts in his closet. He put 3 clean shirts in his drawer. Using this information, which of the following questions could you answer?

Ⓐ How many shirts did Jake put away?
Ⓑ How many shirts does Jake own?
Ⓒ How many of Jake's shirts are dirty?
Ⓓ How many of Jake's shirts are clean?
Ⓔ How many of Jake's shirts can be folded?

15. Pam spent 1 hour cleaning her room. Then she spent 45 minutes sweeping the front porch and 30 minutes dusting the den. After that she read a book for an hour. Finally she helped her mother wash windows for 2 hours. What information is NOT needed to find how much time Pam spent doing chores?

Ⓐ She spent 1 hour cleaning her room.
Ⓑ She swept the porch for 45 minutes.
Ⓒ It took 30 minutes to dust the den.
Ⓓ She read a book for 1 hour.
Ⓔ She spent 2 hours washing windows.

Number Correct/Total = _____ /15

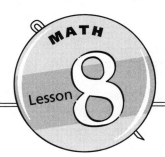

Geometric Figures

Recognizing geometric figures and their features

Directions: Choose the best answer for each question.

A Which figure is a square?

B Which figure is a cylinder?

Example A asks you to find the square in a group of **plane** (flat) **figures**. A **square** is a figure with four sides of equal length and four right angles. Choice Ⓐ has only three sides. It is a **triangle**. Choice Ⓑ is a **circle**. Choice Ⓒ looks something like a square, but you can see that its sides do not have equal length. It is a **rectangle**. Choice Ⓓ is called an **octagon**, because it has eight sides. Choice Ⓔ is a square. It has four sides of equal length and four right angles.

Example B asks you to find the cylinder in a group of **solid figures**. A **cylinder** is a solid shape that has circles for bases. A soup can is a cylinder. Choice Ⓐ is a cylinder. The other choices Ⓑ - Ⓔ are, in order: a **sphere**, a **cone**, a **cube**, and a **pyramid**.

Now look at some more test question examples on page 130.

C What is the perimeter of the shape below?

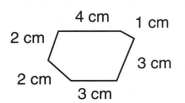

Ⓐ 12 cm   Ⓓ 30 cm

Ⓑ 15 cm   Ⓔ NG

Ⓒ 18 cm

D What is the area of this shape?

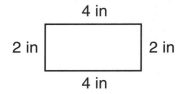

Ⓐ 16 sq in   Ⓓ 6 sq in

Ⓑ 12 sq in   Ⓔ NG

Ⓒ 8 sq in

These examples are about measuring shapes. Example C asks you to find the **perimeter** of the shape. The perimeter of a shape is the length around, or the sum of, all its sides. To find the perimeter of the shape in the example, add $3 + 3 + 2 + 2 + 1 + 4$ to get 15 cm. Choice Ⓑ is correct.

Example D asks you to find the area of the shape. **Area** is the space that is taken up by the shape. Area is a square measure, so the answer is usually given in square units (sq in, sq ft, cm^2, m^2). To find the area, multiply *length × width*. In Example B, this means that you multiply $4 × 2$ to get 8 square inches. Choice Ⓒ is correct.

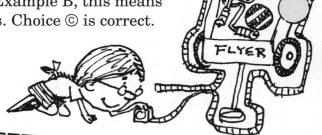

Hint

You can practice your geometry skills at home. Look at objects around your home. Identify each object by shape. Also, try measuring the perimeter and area of each room.

Test-Taking Tips

1 Look for key words and numbers to answer each question. (In Example C, the key word is *perimeter*.)

2 Look at the pictures carefully to help you find the answer. (In Example C, the picture gives the measurement of each side.)

3 Draw your own picture if it will help you answer the question.

 Go for it

Test Practice 8: Geometric Figures

Time: **10** minutes

Directions: Choose the best answer for each question.

1. Which shape is a rectangle?

   Ⓐ   Ⓓ

   Ⓑ    Ⓔ

   Ⓒ

2. How many angles does this shape have?

   Ⓐ 6   Ⓓ 2
   Ⓑ 4   Ⓔ NG
   Ⓒ 3

3. Which figure is a circle?

   Ⓐ    Ⓓ

   Ⓑ   Ⓔ

   Ⓒ

4. Which shape is a cone?

   Ⓐ   Ⓓ

   Ⓑ   Ⓔ

   Ⓒ

5. Which pair of figures has the same size and shape?

   Ⓐ    Ⓓ

   Ⓑ 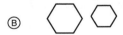   Ⓔ

   Ⓒ

6. Which figure can be folded along the line so that its parts exactly match?

   Ⓐ   Ⓓ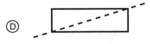

   Ⓑ   Ⓔ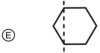

   Ⓒ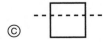

7. Which two figures have the same size and shape?

Ⓐ   Ⓓ

Ⓑ Ⓔ

Ⓒ

8. Which shape can be folded along the line so that its parts exactly match?

Ⓐ Ⓓ

Ⓑ Ⓔ

Ⓒ

9. What is the perimeter of this figure?

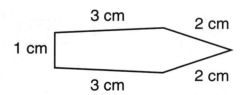

3 cm   2 cm
1 cm
3 cm   2 cm

Ⓐ   6 cm   Ⓓ 12 cm
Ⓑ   7 cm   Ⓔ NG
Ⓒ 11 cm

10. Find the perimeter.

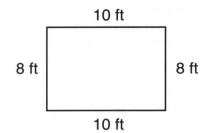

10 ft
8 ft   8 ft
10 ft

Ⓐ 18 sq ft   Ⓓ 80 sq ft
Ⓑ 28 sq ft   Ⓔ NG
Ⓒ 36 sq ft

11. What is the area of this garden plot?

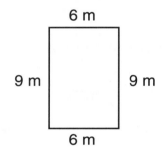

6 m
9 m   9 m
6 m

Ⓐ 15 m²   Ⓓ 54 m²
Ⓑ 30 m²   Ⓔ NG
Ⓒ 48 m²

12. What is the area of this figure in square units?

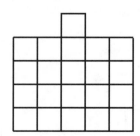

Ⓐ 20   Ⓓ 25
Ⓑ 21   Ⓔ NG
Ⓒ 22

 STOP

Number Correct/Total = _____ /12

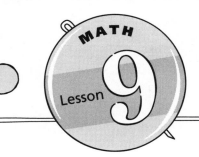

Measurement

Using metric and standard measures, telling time, and recognizing money

Directions: Choose the best answer for each question.

A What is the value of these coins?

Ⓐ 32¢   Ⓒ 35¢

Ⓑ 33¢   Ⓓ 37¢

B What time does this clock say?

Ⓐ 12:45   Ⓒ 1:45

Ⓑ 1:15   Ⓓ 1:55

Example A asks you to identify the amount of money shown in the picture. The picture shows 3 dimes, 1 nickel, and 2 pennies. Each dime is worth 10 cents, so 3 dimes are worth 30¢ (3 × 10 = 30). The nickel is worth 5 cents. Each penny is worth 1 cent, so 2 pennies are worth 2 cents. Now add up these amounts: 30 + 5 + 2 = 37. Choice Ⓓ is correct. The coins in the picture add up to 37¢.

To answer the question in Example B, read the clock carefully. The small hand is pointing to the 1. That means that the hour shown is 1:00. Now you must figure out how many minutes past 1:00 it is. The clock can be divided into quarters, each 15 minutes long. When the big hand points to the 3, it is 15 minutes past the hour. When it points to the 6, it is 30 minutes past the hour. In Example B, the big hand is pointing to the 9. That means it is 45 minutes past the hour. Choice Ⓒ, *1:45*, is the time the clock shows.

Now look at some more test question examples on page 134.

C Which unit is best used to measure how much a person weighs?

Ⓐ meter   Ⓒ gram

Ⓑ kilogram   Ⓓ centimeter

D Two feet equals how many inches?

Ⓐ 6   Ⓒ 20

Ⓑ 12   Ⓓ 24

These kinds of questions deal with two different systems of measurement: the **metric system** and the **standard system**. To answer Example C, you must know the units of measurement in the metric system. In the metric system, weight is measured by grams and kilograms. A gram is very small. It is much easier to measure a person's weight in kilograms than in grams, so choice Ⓑ is correct.

Example D deals with the standard system of measurement. The question in Example D asks you to change feet to inches. There are 12 inches in 1 foot, so there are 24 inches in 2 feet. Choice Ⓓ is correct.

Math Pointers

Metric System	Standard System
Weight	**Weight**
1 kilogram (kg) = 1,000 gm	16 ounces (oz) = 1 pound (lb)
1 metric ton = 1,000 kg	2,000 lb = 1 ton
Length	**Length**
1 meter (m) = 100 centimeters (cm)	1 foot (ft) = 12 inches (in)
1 kilometer (km) = 1,000 m	1 yard (yd) = 3 ft = 36 in
	1 mile = 1,760 yd = 5,280 ft
Volume or Capacity	**Volume or Capacity**
1 liter (l) = 100 centiliters (cl)	1 cup = 8 oz
1 kiloliter (kl) = 1,000 liters	1 pint (pt) = 2 cups = 16 oz
	1 quart (qt) = 2 pt = 32 oz
	1 gallon (gal) = 4 qt = 128 oz

Test-Taking Tips

1 Look for key words and numbers in each question. (In Example C, the key word is *weighs*. This lets you know that you should look for a unit of weight.)

2 Get to know the units of measurement in both the metric and standard systems.

Go for r

Test Practice ⑨: Measurement

Time: 20 minutes

Directions: Choose the best answer for each question.

1. How much money are these bills and coins worth?

ⓐ $3.95

ⓒ $11.95

ⓑ $11.85

ⓓ $20.77

2. Ann had $6.50 in her wallet. She bought a game that cost $6.35. Which picture shows how much money Ann has left in her wallet?

ⓐ ⓒ ⓑ ⓓ

3. What time does this clock say?

ⓐ 10:20

ⓒ 10:40

ⓑ 10:25

ⓓ 11:04

4. What time does this clock say?

ⓐ 9:00

ⓒ 8:45

ⓑ 8:50

ⓓ 8:10

5. Carl left home at 7:30. It took him 15 minutes to ride his bike to school. Which clock shows what time Carl got to school?

ⓐ ⓒ

ⓑ ⓓ

6. Fran's softball game lasted 2 hours. It ended at 1:00. Which clock shows what time it began?

ⓐ ⓒ

ⓑ ⓓ

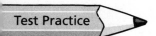
7. What temperature does this thermometer show?

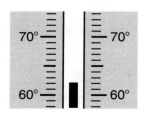

Ⓐ 72°   Ⓒ 63°
Ⓑ 67°   Ⓓ 62°

8. If the temperature rose 6°, what temperature would this thermometer read?

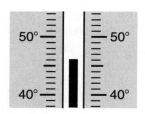

Ⓐ 40°   Ⓒ 52°
Ⓑ 46°   Ⓓ 54°

9. Which unit is best used to measure how long it takes to brush your teeth?

Ⓐ minute   Ⓒ meter
Ⓑ hour   Ⓓ inch

10. Which unit is best used to measure how old you are?

Ⓐ day   Ⓒ month
Ⓑ week   Ⓓ year

11. Which unit is best used to measure how far it is from one side of a playground to another?

Ⓐ inch   Ⓒ yard
Ⓑ ton   Ⓓ mile

12. Which unit is best used to measure how much is in a bottle of juice?

Ⓐ liter   Ⓒ centimeter
Ⓑ kilogram   Ⓓ kiloliter

13. How long is this piece of rope?

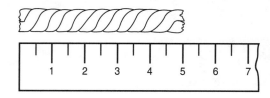

Ⓐ 5.0   Ⓒ 6.0
Ⓑ 5.5   Ⓓ 6.5

14. How long is this hair clip?

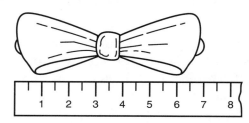

Ⓐ 6.0 cm   Ⓒ 7.0 cm
Ⓑ 6.5 cm   Ⓓ 7.5 cm

15. Sid is 54 inches tall. How many feet tall is he?

Ⓐ 3.5 ft   Ⓒ 4.5 ft
Ⓑ 4.0 ft   Ⓓ 5.0 ft

16. 10 kilograms =

Ⓐ 100 milligrams
Ⓑ 1000 grams
Ⓒ 1000 milligrams
Ⓓ 10,000 grams

Number Correct/Total = _____ /16

Interpreting Data

Reading and interpreting calendars,
tables, charts, and graphs

Directions: This bar graph shows the number of
children who chose each TV show as their favorite.
Use the graph to answer each question.

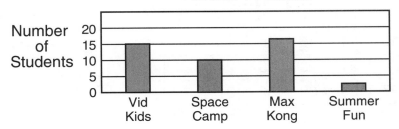

Favorite TV Shows

A How many children
chose "Space Camp" as
their favorite show?

Ⓐ 5   Ⓒ 15

Ⓑ 10   Ⓓ 20

B Which is the most
popular show?

Ⓐ "Vid Kids"

Ⓑ "Space Camp"

Ⓒ "Max Kong"

Ⓓ "Summer Fun"

To answer Example A, find the name "Space Camp"
at the bottom of the graph. Look at the bar. Then find
the number on the left side at the same level as the top
of the bar. The correct answer is choice Ⓑ, *10*.

In Example C, look for the highest bar. Choice Ⓒ,
"Max Kong," is correct.

Hint

Try looking through the
magazines and newspapers in
your home, or at the library. See
if you can find charts, graphs,
or tables. Then practice reading
the information. You might
even want to try making your
own graphs and charts, to help
you understand how they are
put together.

Test-Taking Tips

1 Look for the key words in each
question (such as *most, least, how
many*, and *in all*.)

2 Look back at the graph
or chart to answer
each question.

Go for it

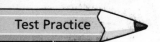

Test Practice 10 : Interpreting Data   Time: 12 minutes

Questions 1–3. Use the calendar below to answer each question.

MAY						
Sun	Mon	Tue	Wed	Thu	Fri	Sat
		1	2	3	4	5
6	7	8	9	10	11	12
13	14	15	16	17	18	19
20	21	22	23	24	25	26
27	28	29	30	31		

1. What day is May 16?

   Ⓐ Monday
   Ⓑ Tuesday
   Ⓒ Wednesday
   Ⓓ Thursday

2. What date is the third Friday of the month?

   Ⓐ May 11
   Ⓑ May 18
   Ⓒ May 24
   Ⓓ May 25

3. What date is two weeks from May 7?

   Ⓐ May 14
   Ⓑ May 18
   Ⓒ May 20
   Ⓓ May 21

Questions 4–6. The table below shows how many kids went on each ride at the fair. Use the table to answer each question.

Ride	Number of Kids
Merry-Go-Round	||||
Ferris Wheel	⊬⊬⊬
Roller Coaster	⊬⊬⊬ ||
Octopus	⊬⊬⊬ |||

4. How many kids went on the Ferris wheel?

   Ⓐ 4
   Ⓑ 5
   Ⓒ 7
   Ⓓ 8

5. Which ride did the most kids go on?

   Ⓐ Merry-Go-Round
   Ⓑ Ferris Wheel
   Ⓒ Roller Coaster
   Ⓓ Octopus

6. Which ride had the fewest riders?

   Ⓐ Merry-Go-Round
   Ⓑ Ferris Wheel
   Ⓒ Roller Coaster
   Ⓓ Octopus

GO ON

Questions 7–9. The bar graph below shows the number of kids from each state who went to a summer camp. Use the graph to answer each question.

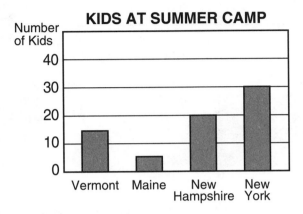

KIDS AT SUMMER CAMP

7. How many kids came from Maine?

   Ⓐ 5
   Ⓑ 10
   Ⓒ 15
   Ⓓ 20

8. The most campers came from which state?

   Ⓐ Vermont
   Ⓑ Maine
   Ⓒ New Hampshire
   Ⓓ New York

9. How many more kids came from New Hampshire than from Maine?

   Ⓐ 5
   Ⓑ 10
   Ⓒ 15
   Ⓓ 20

Questions 10–12. The chart below shows how many colored T-shirts each child has. Use the chart to answer each question.

COLORED T-SHIRTS

Name	Red	Blue	Yellow	Black
Jody	2	3	0	1
Sam	0	1	0	4
Marta	1	2	2	2
Colin	3	1	1	0

10. How many blue T-shirts does Jody have?

    Ⓐ 0
    Ⓑ 1
    Ⓒ 2
    Ⓓ 3

11. Who has the most black T-shirts?

    Ⓐ Jody
    Ⓑ Sam
    Ⓒ Marta
    Ⓓ Colin

12. Who has the most T-shirts in all?

    Ⓐ Jody
    Ⓑ Sam
    Ⓒ Marta
    Ⓓ Colin

Number Correct/Total = _____ /12

*This test will tell you how well you might score on a standardized math test **after** using this book. If you compare your scores on Tryout Tests 1 and 2, you'll see how much you've learned!*

Math Tryout Test 2

Time: **30** minutes

Directions: Choose the best answer for each question. Fill in the circle beside the answer you choose. The answer to the sample question (**S**) has been filled in for you.

S Which numeral means one thousand fifty?

- Ⓐ 1500
- Ⓑ 1005
- ● 1050
- Ⓓ 150

1. What is another name for 410?

- Ⓐ 4 hundreds and 1 one
- Ⓑ 3 hundreds and 11 tens
- Ⓒ 3 hundreds and 11 ones
- Ⓓ 4 hundreds and 10 tens

2. Which number sentence is true?

- Ⓐ 212 > 122
- Ⓑ 121 < 112
- Ⓒ 211 > 212
- Ⓓ 122 < 121

3. Which numeral has 6 tens and 5 ones?

- Ⓐ 56
- Ⓒ 560
- Ⓑ 650
- Ⓓ 65

4. Which group of numbers is in order from least to greatest?

- Ⓐ 412, 193, 301
- Ⓑ 193, 301, 412
- Ⓒ 301, 412, 193
- Ⓓ 412, 301, 193

5. Which animal is 3rd in line?

Ⓐ   Ⓑ   Ⓒ   Ⓓ

6. Each shelf has 10 books. How many books are there in all?

- Ⓐ 6
- Ⓒ 40
- Ⓑ 24
- Ⓓ 42

7. What is 1483 rounded to the nearest ten?

- Ⓐ 1500
- Ⓒ 1485
- Ⓑ 1490
- Ⓓ 1480

8. Which number is missing in the pattern below?

151, 250, 349, _____

- Ⓐ 452
- Ⓒ 448
- Ⓑ 450
- Ⓓ 438

GO ON

9. Which group has only odd numbers?

   Ⓐ 2, 6, 20
   Ⓑ 1, 9, 15
   Ⓒ 3, 12, 19
   Ⓓ 8, 13, 21

10. Which number is closest to

    $88 - 41$?

    Ⓐ 40
    Ⓑ 43
    Ⓒ 50
    Ⓓ 55

11. Which two pictures have the same fraction shaded?

    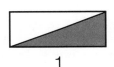

    Ⓐ pictures 1 and 3
    Ⓑ pictures 2 and 4
    Ⓒ pictures 3 and 4
    Ⓓ pictures 2 and 3

12. Which is another name for $\frac{9}{12}$?

    Ⓐ $\frac{3}{4}$
    Ⓑ $\frac{4}{3}$
    Ⓒ $\frac{2}{3}$
    Ⓓ $\frac{3}{6}$

13. Which decimal is greater than .05?

    Ⓐ .20
    Ⓑ .04
    Ⓒ .006
    Ⓓ .01

14. Which number sentence shows how many chairs there are in all?

    Ⓐ $4 \times 3 = 12$
    Ⓑ $4 - 3 = 1$
    Ⓒ $7 - 4 = 3$
    Ⓓ $4 + 3 = 7$

15. Which number best completes this number sentence?

    $8 \times \square = 24$

    Ⓐ 2   Ⓒ 4
    Ⓑ 3   Ⓓ 6

16. Which number makes both of these number sentences true?

    $6 + 12 = 12 + \square$

    $12 \times (3 \times 6) = (12 \times 3) \times \square$

    Ⓐ 0   Ⓒ 6
    Ⓑ 3   Ⓓ 12

141

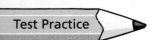

Math Tryout Test 2 (continued)

Directions: Choose the best answer for each question.

17. 611
    + 329

Ⓐ 930
Ⓑ 938
Ⓒ 940
Ⓓ 950
Ⓔ NG

18. 283
    − 44

Ⓐ 149
Ⓑ 239
Ⓒ 241
Ⓓ 247
Ⓔ NG

19. 572
    × 4

Ⓐ 2008
Ⓑ 2288
Ⓒ 2308
Ⓓ 2388
Ⓔ NG

20. 12)‾144‾

Ⓐ 10
Ⓑ 11
Ⓒ 13
Ⓓ 14
Ⓔ NG

21. $1\frac{3}{8} + \frac{1}{8} =$

Ⓐ $\frac{4}{8}$
Ⓑ $1\frac{1}{4}$
Ⓒ $1\frac{1}{2}$
Ⓓ $1\frac{5}{8}$
Ⓔ NG

22. $12.29
    − 4.50

Ⓐ $8.79
Ⓑ $8.69
Ⓒ $8.59
Ⓓ $7.79
Ⓔ $7.39

23. Matt had 15 markers. He bought 9 more. How many does he have in all?

Ⓐ 24   Ⓓ 6
Ⓑ 23   Ⓔ NG
Ⓒ 8

24. Bo makes $30 a week on her paper route. Last week she also got $5 tips from 4 people. How much did Bo make last week in all?

Ⓐ $10   Ⓓ $50
Ⓑ $20   Ⓔ NG
Ⓒ $40

25. Tanya wrote 2 letters every day for 4 days. Which number sentence could you use to find out how many she wrote in all?

Ⓐ $2 \times 4 = \square$ Ⓓ $4 \div 2 = \square$
Ⓑ $4 - 2 = \square$ Ⓔ NG
Ⓒ $2 + 4 = \square$

26. Each of the Mendez sisters invited 4 friends to a party. What other information do you need to find out how many people the sisters invited?

Ⓐ how many people are in the Mendez family
Ⓑ what time the party was
Ⓒ where the party was held
Ⓓ whether the sisters have any brothers
Ⓔ how many Mendez sisters there are

GO ON

27. Which figure is a triangle?

Ⓐ   Ⓓ

Ⓑ 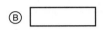   Ⓔ NG

Ⓒ

28. Which of the following is a cube?

Ⓐ 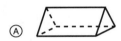   Ⓓ

Ⓑ   Ⓔ NG

Ⓒ

29. Which of these figures has a line of symmetry?

Ⓐ   Ⓒ

Ⓑ   Ⓓ

30. What is the perimeter of the field pictured below?

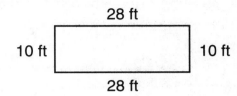

Ⓐ 18 ft   Ⓓ 280 ft
Ⓑ 56 ft   Ⓔ NG
Ⓒ 76 ft

31. What is the area of this figure in square units?

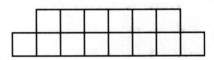

Ⓐ 14   Ⓓ 18
Ⓑ 15   Ⓔ NG
Ⓒ 16

32. What is the total value of the coins shown?

Ⓐ $1.50   Ⓓ $1.23
Ⓑ $1.38   Ⓔ NG
Ⓒ $1.28

Math Tryout Test 2 (continued)

33. Tamara got to the zoo at 10:15. She spent 5 hours there. Which clock shows what time she left the zoo?

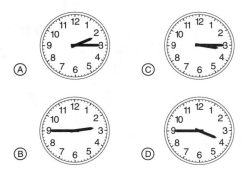

The chart below shows the numbers of cans of food brought in by each grade at King School during a food drive. Use the chart to answer questions 36–38.

Grade	Soup	Vegetables	Meat
1	20	31	14
2	8	33	19
3	24	25	23
4	19	24	26

34. How tall is this boy?

Ⓐ 36 in

Ⓑ 42 in

Ⓒ 44 in

Ⓓ 48 in

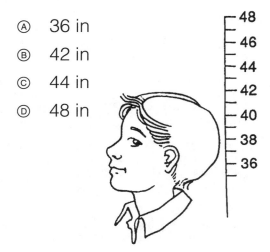

36. Which grade brought in the greatest number of cans of food for the food drive?

Ⓐ Grade 1   Ⓒ Grade 3

Ⓑ Grade 2   Ⓓ Grade 4

37. Which grade brought in more cans of meat than of vegetables?

Ⓐ Grade 1   Ⓒ Grade 3

Ⓑ Grade 2   Ⓓ Grade 4

35. 1 meter =

Ⓐ 1000 millimeters

Ⓑ 10 kilometers

Ⓒ 100 grams

Ⓓ 1000 centimeters

38. How many cans of food did the first graders bring in all?

Ⓐ 51   Ⓒ 64

Ⓑ 60   Ⓓ 65

Number Correct/Total = _____ /38

Some Things Parents Want To Know About Standardized Tests

Why are national standardized tests sometimes called "high stakes" tests?

Your child's test scores are often used to "track" him or her into a particular educational program. If a child scores well, opportunities for special programs and teachers frequently become available. If scores are low, the child may be marked as a slow student and placed in a program or group that limits the chance to develop. Elementary school standardized tests can actually shape a child's high school program —as well as affect chances for a college education. These are "high stakes" indeed!

How will this book help my child get better test scores?

It will help your child in two ways: one, all the test questions in this study guide focus *exclusively* on the very same skills and content areas tested by the five most widely used standardized tests—your child will learn exactly what he or she needs to know to get better test scores. Two, this study guide provides intensive practice in important and effective test-taking strategies.

How often are national standardized tests given at my child's school?

Most schools give national standardized tests yearly. Usually, they are given in the spring or fall—and in some schools both times. Check with your school to get your child's test dates.

What are standardized tests used for?

The tests are designed to measure the effectiveness of your child's school, and at the same time to identify your child's strengths and weaknesses in reading, language arts, and math. The school's scores can help you learn how well your school is teaching these subjects compared to other schools around the nation and other schools in your own school district.

Why does this book span two grade levels?

Each of the five national standardized tests on which this study guide is based covers two grade levels. It is possible that your child will encounter questions in this guide and on the standardized test that cover content he or she has not yet had. Not to worry: this study guide can provide advance preparation for the content your child will be required to know later this year or next year. Moreover, your child's scores on the standardized tests are adjusted to reflect his or her actual grade level. In any case, the national tests do not expect 100% correct answers or 100% completion of all the test questions—and you needn't either.

When should my child start using this book?

Using this book throughout the school year can be very helpful, since classroom teachers give tests on an average of three out of every five school days. To prepare for the national standardized test covering reading, language arts, and math, spend a few hours each week for about six to eight weeks before the test date.

Should I expect my child to work independently in this book?

This guide is designed for independent study. However, some children may need help getting started, so you'll want to get familiar with the guide's format and content. You'll probably want to show your child how this study guide can help. Work together to set up a regular, and realistic, study schedule. It is important to allow your child to self-score all the tests. This encourages the child to take responsibility for his or her progress and builds confidence that will carry over to school work.

Answer Keys

Use these answer keys to count up the number correct on each test.

Reading Tryout Test 1

page 9

1. Ⓐ
2. Ⓒ
3. Ⓑ
4. Ⓒ
5. Ⓐ
6. Ⓑ
7. Ⓒ
8. Ⓒ
9. Ⓐ
10. Ⓑ
11. Ⓑ
12. Ⓐ
13. Ⓒ
14. Ⓒ

page 10

15. Ⓒ
16. Ⓐ
17. Ⓓ
18. Ⓑ
19. Ⓑ
20. Ⓓ
21. Ⓑ
22. Ⓐ
23. Ⓒ
24. Ⓓ

page 11

25. Ⓑ
26. Ⓐ
27. Ⓓ
28. Ⓑ

page 12

29. Ⓒ
30. Ⓑ
31. Ⓐ
32. Ⓒ

page 13

33. Ⓒ
34. Ⓓ
35. Ⓐ
36. Ⓓ

Test Practice 1
Consonant Sounds

page 15

1. Ⓐ
2. Ⓑ
3. Ⓐ
4. Ⓒ
5. Ⓑ
6. Ⓑ
7. Ⓑ
8. Ⓒ
9. Ⓑ
10. Ⓐ
11. Ⓑ
12. Ⓒ
13. Ⓐ
14. Ⓐ
15. Ⓑ

Test Practice 2
Vowel Sounds

page 17

1. Ⓑ
2. Ⓒ
3. Ⓐ
4. Ⓒ
5. Ⓐ
6. Ⓐ
7. Ⓑ
8. Ⓑ
9. Ⓐ
10. Ⓑ
11. Ⓑ
12. Ⓒ
13. Ⓑ
14. Ⓒ
15. Ⓑ

Test Practice 3
Prefixes, Suffixes, and Root Words

page 19

1. Ⓑ
2. Ⓐ
3. Ⓓ
4. Ⓒ
5. Ⓓ
6. Ⓐ
7. Ⓒ
8. Ⓐ
9. Ⓑ
10. Ⓒ
11. Ⓐ
12. Ⓓ

Test Practice 4
Compound Words and Contractions

page 21

1. Ⓐ
2. Ⓑ
3. Ⓒ
4. Ⓑ
5. Ⓓ
6. Ⓒ
7. Ⓓ
8. Ⓐ
9. Ⓐ
10. Ⓒ
11. Ⓓ
12. Ⓒ
13. Ⓓ
14. Ⓐ

Test Practice 5
Word Meaning

page 23

1. Ⓐ
2. Ⓒ
3. Ⓑ
4. Ⓓ
5. Ⓑ
6. Ⓓ
7. Ⓐ
8. Ⓓ
9. Ⓒ
10. Ⓓ
11. Ⓐ
12. Ⓑ

Test Practice 6
Synonyms and Antonyms

page 25

1. Ⓑ
2. Ⓐ
3. Ⓒ
4. Ⓓ
5. Ⓐ
6. Ⓑ
7. Ⓒ
8. Ⓒ
9. Ⓓ
10. Ⓒ

Test Practice 7
Context Clues

page 27

1. Ⓐ	6. Ⓒ
2. Ⓒ	7. Ⓓ
3. Ⓑ	8. Ⓐ
4. Ⓓ	9. Ⓓ
5. Ⓐ	10. Ⓑ

Test Practice 8
Main Idea and Details

pages 30–31

1. Ⓒ	5. Ⓒ
2. Ⓒ	6. Ⓓ
3. Ⓑ	7. Ⓒ
4. Ⓓ	8. Ⓑ

Test Practice 9
Constructing Meaning

pages 34–35

1. Ⓑ	6. Ⓑ
2. Ⓓ	7. Ⓒ
3. Ⓐ	8. Ⓐ
4. Ⓓ	9. Ⓑ
5. Ⓑ	10. Ⓐ

Test Practice 10
Evaluating Information

page 38

1. Ⓓ	3. Ⓓ
2. Ⓑ	4. Ⓑ

page 39

5. Ⓒ	7. Ⓑ
6. Ⓐ	8. Ⓓ

Test Practice 11
Characters and Plot

pages 42–43

1. Ⓑ	6. Ⓓ
2. Ⓑ	7. Ⓒ
3. Ⓐ	8. Ⓐ
4. Ⓒ	9. Ⓑ
5. Ⓒ	10. Ⓓ

Test Practice 12
Reading Literature

pages 46–47

1. Ⓓ	5. Ⓑ
2. Ⓒ	6. Ⓐ
3. Ⓒ	7. Ⓑ
4. Ⓑ	8. Ⓓ

Reading Tryout Test 2

page 48

1. Ⓑ	8. Ⓒ
2. Ⓑ	9. Ⓐ
3. Ⓒ	10. Ⓑ
4. Ⓐ	11. Ⓑ
5. Ⓒ	12. Ⓐ
6. Ⓐ	13. Ⓒ
7. Ⓑ	14. Ⓐ

page 49

15. Ⓐ	20. Ⓐ
16. Ⓑ	21. Ⓑ
17. Ⓓ	22. Ⓒ
18. Ⓒ	23. Ⓓ
19. Ⓒ	24. Ⓐ

page 50

25. Ⓓ	27. Ⓑ
26. Ⓑ	28. Ⓓ

page 51

29. Ⓑ	31. Ⓒ
30. Ⓑ	32. Ⓓ

page 52

33. Ⓐ	35. Ⓑ
34. Ⓒ	36. Ⓓ

Answer Keys

Use these answer keys to count up the number correct on each test.

Language Arts Tryout Test 1

page 55
1. Ⓐ
2. Ⓑ
3. Ⓓ
4. Ⓓ
5. Ⓐ
6. Ⓑ
7. Ⓐ

page 56
8. Ⓒ
9. Ⓑ
10. Ⓓ
11. Ⓑ
12. Ⓒ
13. Ⓐ

page 57
14. Ⓒ
15. Ⓐ
16. Ⓐ
17. Ⓓ
18. Ⓒ
19. Ⓐ

page 58
20. Ⓒ
21. Ⓑ
22. Ⓓ
23. Ⓑ
24. Ⓐ
25. Ⓒ
26. Ⓒ
27. Ⓐ

page 59
28. Ⓑ
29. Ⓓ
30. Ⓑ
31. Ⓒ
32. Ⓒ
33. Ⓐ
34. Ⓓ
35. Ⓑ

Test Practice 1
Parts of Speech

page 62
1. Ⓐ
2. Ⓓ
3. Ⓒ
4. Ⓑ
5. Ⓐ
6. Ⓐ
7. Ⓒ
8. Ⓓ
9. Ⓑ
10. Ⓒ

page 63
11. Ⓑ
12. Ⓓ
13. Ⓒ
14. Ⓑ
15. Ⓐ
16. Ⓑ
17. Ⓓ
18. Ⓐ

Test Practice 2
Sentence Parts

page 65
1. Ⓐ
2. Ⓑ
3. Ⓑ
4. Ⓐ
5. Ⓐ
6. Ⓑ
7. Ⓒ
8. Ⓑ
9. Ⓒ
10. Ⓑ
11. Ⓑ
12. Ⓒ

page 66
13. Ⓒ
14. Ⓐ
15. Ⓒ
16. Ⓑ
17. Ⓒ
18. Ⓑ
19. Ⓐ
20. Ⓑ
21. Ⓐ
22. Ⓒ

Test Practice 3
Sentences

pages 68–69
1. Ⓒ
2. Ⓑ
3. Ⓐ
4. Ⓐ
5. Ⓓ
6. Ⓓ
7. Ⓑ
8. Ⓒ
9. Ⓓ
10. Ⓐ
11. Ⓑ
12. Ⓓ
13. Ⓒ
14. Ⓓ
15. Ⓒ
16. Ⓑ

Test Practice 4
Combining Sentences

pages 71–72
1. Ⓑ
2. Ⓓ
3. Ⓑ
4. Ⓒ
5. Ⓐ
6. Ⓒ
7. Ⓐ
8. Ⓑ
9. Ⓐ
10. Ⓓ

Test Practice 5
Writing Paragraphs

pages 74–75
1. Ⓓ
2. Ⓐ
3. Ⓑ
4. Ⓐ
5. Ⓐ
6. Ⓒ
7. Ⓓ
8. Ⓒ

Test Practice 6
Spelling

page 77

1.	D	9.	C
2.	A	10.	B
3.	D	11.	D
4.	C	12.	A
5.	A	13.	D
6.	B	14.	A
7.	D	15.	C
8.	B		

page 78

16.	B	21.	B
17.	C	22.	C
18.	B	23.	D
19.	A	24.	A
20.	C	25.	B

Test Practice 7
Punctuation

page 81

1.	B	6.	A
2.	A	7.	D
3.	C	8.	A
4.	B	9.	D
5.	D	10.	C

page 82

11.	A	14.	D
12.	A	15.	D
13.	B	16.	B

Test Practice 8
Capitalization

page 84

1.	D	6.	A
2.	B	7.	D
3.	C	8.	C
4.	C	9.	B
5.	A	10.	D

page 85

11.	B	14.	C
12.	D	15.	A
13.	A	16.	C

Test Practice 9
Research Skills

page 87

1.	A	8.	C
2.	D	9.	D
3.	A	10.	A
4.	B	11.	A
5.	C	12.	B
6.	D	13.	D
7.	C	14.	D

Test Practice 10
Reference Sources

page 89

1.	D	4.	D
2.	B	5.	C
3.	A		

page 90

6.	D	10.	C
7.	A	11.	A
8.	D	12.	D
9.	B		

Test Practice 11
Maps, Charts, and Graphs

page 92   **page 93**

1.	C	7.	D
2.	B	8.	B
3.	C	9.	C
4.	A	10.	B
5.	C	11.	A
6.	D	12.	C

Language Arts Tryout Test 2

page 94

1.	A	5.	A
2.	B	6.	A
3.	D	7.	B
4.	D		

page 95

8.	B	11.	B
9.	C	12.	B
10.	D	13.	A

page 96

14.	C	17.	B
15.	A	18.	C
16.	A	19.	A

page 97

20.	C	24.	A
21.	B	25.	C
22.	D	26.	D
23.	C	27.	A

page 98

28.	B	32.	B
29.	D	33.	D
30.	B	34.	B
31.	D	35.	C

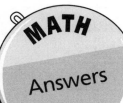

MATH Answers

Answer Keys

Use these answer keys to count up the number correct on each test.

Math Tryout Test 1

page 101

1. Ⓓ   5. Ⓓ
2. Ⓑ   6. Ⓐ
3. Ⓒ   7. Ⓑ
4. Ⓒ   8. Ⓒ

page 102

9. Ⓐ   13. Ⓒ
10. Ⓓ   14. Ⓓ
11. Ⓓ   15. Ⓑ
12. Ⓐ   16. Ⓐ

page 103

17. Ⓒ   22. Ⓓ
18. Ⓑ   23. Ⓑ
19. Ⓐ   24. Ⓒ
20. Ⓑ   25. Ⓐ
21. Ⓔ   26. Ⓓ

page 104

27. Ⓓ   30. Ⓒ
28. Ⓐ   31. Ⓐ
29. Ⓒ   32. Ⓐ

page 105

33. Ⓒ   36. Ⓒ
34. Ⓐ   37. Ⓑ
35. Ⓑ   38. Ⓐ

Test Practice 1
Whole Number Concepts

page 108

1. Ⓐ   5. Ⓑ
2. Ⓒ   6. Ⓓ
3. Ⓑ   7. Ⓑ
4. Ⓓ   8. Ⓑ

page 109

9. Ⓒ   13. Ⓑ
10. Ⓓ   14. Ⓒ
11. Ⓒ   15. Ⓓ
12. Ⓒ   16. Ⓓ

page 110

17. Ⓐ   21. Ⓓ
18. Ⓑ   22. Ⓒ
19. Ⓑ   23. Ⓐ
20. Ⓓ   24. Ⓓ

Test Practice 2
Fractions and Decimals

page 112

1. Ⓓ   6. Ⓓ
2. Ⓑ   7. Ⓒ
3. Ⓓ   8. Ⓐ
4. Ⓓ   9. Ⓑ
5. Ⓒ   10. Ⓑ

Test Practice 3
Using Numbers

page 114

1. Ⓐ   5. Ⓐ
2. Ⓒ   6. Ⓓ
3. Ⓓ   7. Ⓒ
4. Ⓐ

Test Practice 3
(continued)

page 115

8. Ⓒ   13. Ⓐ
9. Ⓒ   14. Ⓑ
10. Ⓓ   15. Ⓐ
11. Ⓐ   16. Ⓒ
12. Ⓓ

Test Practice 4
Addition and Subtraction

page 117

1. Ⓒ   7. Ⓐ
2. Ⓓ   8. Ⓓ
3. Ⓑ   9. Ⓔ
4. Ⓑ   10. Ⓐ
5. Ⓔ   12. Ⓑ
6. Ⓒ   12. Ⓓ

page 118

13. Ⓑ   19. Ⓐ
14. Ⓓ   20. Ⓔ
15. Ⓒ   21. Ⓓ
16. Ⓑ   22. Ⓐ
17. Ⓒ   23. Ⓑ
18. Ⓑ   24. Ⓓ

Test Practice 5
Multiplication and Division

page 120

1.	Ⓒ	6.	Ⓓ
2.	Ⓐ	7.	Ⓐ
3.	Ⓑ	8.	Ⓒ
4.	Ⓓ	9.	Ⓓ
5.	Ⓓ	10.	Ⓑ

page 121

11.	Ⓓ	17.	Ⓑ
12.	Ⓒ	18.	Ⓒ
13.	Ⓒ	19.	Ⓔ
14.	Ⓐ	20.	Ⓓ
15.	Ⓒ	21.	Ⓐ
16.	Ⓑ	22.	Ⓒ

Test Practice 6
Working with Fractions and Decimals

page 123

1.	Ⓐ	6.	Ⓐ
2.	Ⓓ	7.	Ⓑ
3.	Ⓐ	8.	Ⓒ
4.	Ⓔ	9.	Ⓓ
5.	Ⓓ	10.	Ⓔ

page 124

11.	Ⓒ	16.	Ⓔ
12.	Ⓑ	17.	Ⓑ
13.	Ⓒ	18.	Ⓓ
14.	Ⓐ	19.	Ⓓ
15.	Ⓓ	20.	Ⓒ

Test Practice 7
Problem Solving

page 127

1.	Ⓐ	5.	Ⓓ
2.	Ⓓ	6.	Ⓑ
3.	Ⓓ	7.	Ⓓ
4.	Ⓑ	8.	Ⓔ

page 128

9.	Ⓔ	13.	Ⓑ
10.	Ⓑ	14.	Ⓐ
11.	Ⓒ	15.	Ⓓ
12.	Ⓑ		

Test Practice 8
Geometric Figures

page 131

1.	Ⓔ	4.	Ⓔ
2.	Ⓐ	5.	Ⓐ
3.	Ⓓ	6.	Ⓑ

page 132

7.	Ⓒ	10.	Ⓓ
8.	Ⓐ	11.	Ⓓ
9.	Ⓒ	12.	Ⓑ

Test Practice 9
Measurement

page 135

1.	Ⓒ	4.	Ⓑ
2.	Ⓓ	5.	Ⓑ
3.	Ⓐ	6.	Ⓐ

page 136

7.	Ⓓ	12.	Ⓐ
8.	Ⓒ	13.	Ⓐ
9.	Ⓐ	14.	Ⓒ
10.	Ⓓ	15.	Ⓒ
11.	Ⓒ	16.	Ⓓ

Test Practice 10
Interpreting Data

page 138   **page 139**

1.	Ⓒ	7.	Ⓐ
2.	Ⓑ	8.	Ⓓ
3.	Ⓓ	9.	Ⓒ
4.	Ⓑ	10.	Ⓓ
5.	Ⓓ	11.	Ⓑ
6.	Ⓐ	12.	Ⓒ

Math Tryout Test 2

page 140

1.	Ⓑ	5.	Ⓒ
2.	Ⓐ	6.	Ⓓ
3.	Ⓓ	7.	Ⓓ
4.	Ⓑ	8.	Ⓒ

page 141

9.	Ⓑ	13.	Ⓐ
10.	Ⓒ	14.	Ⓓ
11.	Ⓑ	15.	Ⓑ
12.	Ⓐ	16.	Ⓒ

page 142

17.	Ⓒ	22.	Ⓓ
18.	Ⓑ	23.	Ⓐ
19.	Ⓑ	24.	Ⓓ
20.	Ⓔ	25.	Ⓐ
21.	Ⓒ	26.	Ⓔ

page 143

27.	Ⓒ	30.	Ⓒ
28.	Ⓓ	31.	Ⓐ
29.	Ⓐ	32.	Ⓑ

page 144

33.	Ⓒ	36.	Ⓒ
34.	Ⓑ	37.	Ⓓ
35.	Ⓐ	38.	Ⓓ

Finding Percent

Most standardized tests give your score in both number of correct answers and in percentages. This handy chart will tell you your percent score.

1. Find the band with the same number of questions that are on your test.
2. Follow along the top row of the band to the number of correct answers you got. Your Percent Score is right below it.

Number of Questions on Test

8

1	2	3	4	5	6	7	8
13%	25%	38%	50%	63%	75%	88%	100%

10

1	2	3	4	5	6	7	8	9	10
10%	20%	30%	40%	50%	60%	70%	80%	90%	100%

12

1	2	3	4	5	6	7	8	9	10	11	12
8%	17%	25%	33%	42%	50%	58%	67%	75%	83%	92%	100%

14

1	2	3	4	5	6	7	8	9	10	11	12	13	14
7%	14%	21%	29%	36%	43%	50%	57%	64%	71%	79%	86%	93%	100%

15

1	2	3	4	5	6	7	8	9	10	11	12	13	14	15
7%	13%	20%	27%	33%	40%	47%	53%	60%	67%	73%	80%	87%	93%	100%

16

1	2	3	4	5	6	7	8	9	10	11	12	13	14	15	16
6%	13%	19%	25%	31%	38%	44%	50%	56%	63%	69%	75%	81%	88%	94%	100%

18

1	2	3	4	5	6	7	8	9	10	11	12	13	14	15	16	17	18
6%	11%	17%	22%	28%	33%	39%	44%	50%	56%	61%	67%	72%	78%	83%	89%	94%	100%

20

1	2	3	4	5	6	7	8	9	10	11	12	13	14	15	16	17	18	19	20
5%	10%	15%	20%	25%	30%	35%	40%	45%	50%	55%	60%	65%	70%	75%	80%	85%	90%	95%	100%

22

1	2	3	4	5	6	7	8	9	10	11	12	13	14	15	16	17	18	19	20	21	22
5%	9%	14%	18%	23%	27%	32%	36%	41%	45%	50%	55%	59%	64%	68%	73%	77%	82%	86%	91%	95%	100%

24

1	2	3	4	5	6	7	8	9	10	11	12	13	14	15	16	17	18	19	20	21	22	23	24
4%	8%	13%	17%	21%	25%	29%	33%	38%	42%	46%	50%	54%	58%	63%	67%	71%	75%	79%	83%	88%	92%	96%	100%

25

1	2	3	4	5	6	7	8	9	10	11	12	13	14	15	16	17	18	19	20	21	22	23	24	25
4%	8%	12%	16%	20%	24%	28%	32%	36%	40%	44%	48%	52%	56%	60%	64%	68%	72%	76%	80%	84%	88%	92%	96%	100%

35

1	2	3	4	5	6	7	8	9	10	11	12	13	14	15	16	17	18
3%	6%	9%	11%	14%	17%	20%	23%	26%	29%	31%	34%	37%	40%	43%	46%	49%	51%

19	20	21	22	23	24	25	26	27	28	29	30	31	32	33	34	35
54%	57%	60%	63%	66%	69%	71%	74%	77%	80%	83%	86%	89%	91%	94%	97%	100%

36

1	2	3	4	5	6	7	8	9	10	11	12	13	14	15	16	17	18
3%	6%	8%	11%	14%	17%	19%	22%	25%	28%	31%	33%	36%	39%	42%	44%	47%	50%

19	20	21	22	23	24	25	26	27	28	29	30	31	32	33	34	35	36
53%	56%	58%	61%	64%	67%	69%	72%	75%	78%	81%	83%	86%	89%	92%	94%	97%	100%

38

1	2	3	4	5	6	7	8	9	10	11	12	13	14	15	16	17	18	19
3%	5%	8%	11%	13%	16%	18%	21%	24%	26%	29%	32%	34%	37%	39%	42%	45%	47%	50%

20	21	22	23	24	25	26	27	28	29	30	31	32	33	34	35	36	37	38
53%	55%	58%	61%	63%	66%	68%	71%	74%	76%	79%	82%	84%	87%	89%	92%	95%	97%	100%